Christening
cakes

Christening
cakes

Linda Pawsey

MEREHURST

Contents

Introduction   7

Equipment   8

Recipes   10

Preparing the Cakes   14

A Gift for Baby   16

Elegant Storks   19

Teddies' Presents   24

Little Angels   28

Alphabet Heart   33

Up, Up and Away Teddy   36

Modelling a Crib	40	Draped Lace Crib	76
Bib and Blossoms	43	New Arrival	80
Duck's Bathtime	46	Twins' Slumber	84
Making a Splash	50	Chiffon Elegance	88
Dainty Pram	54	Fabric Effects	92
Fit for a Princess	58	Building Blocks	94
Delicate Rose Crib	62	Pink Bootees	97
Modelling Babies	66		
Sleepy Pals	69	Templates	100
Jumbo Junior's Nap	72	Suppliers	108
		Index	110

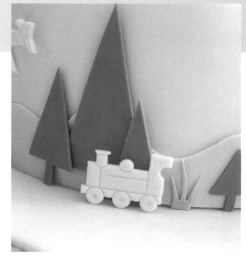

This book is dedicated to Michael Heynes, my husband.

Once in a lifetime you find someone
Who touches not only your heart but also your soul.
Once in a lifetime you find someone
Who stands beside you not over you.
You find someone who loves you
For who you are and not what you could be.
Once in a lifetime
If you are lucky
You find someone
As we have found each other.

Nanci Brilliant

I also dedicate this book to my mum, who very sadly died on January 31st 1999:
a true friend, mentor and loving mum. I miss her every day.

A special thank you to Heather Smith, without whose help this book
would not have been possible, and also thanks to Terry Wood and George Hosgood
at D.I.Y. Icing Centre for their continued support and friendship.

Introduction

The birth of a baby is without doubt a life-changing experience for many, many reasons and it is definitely a time for special celebrations for all the family.

A new baby will probably mean a lot less time for extravagant pastimes such as cake decorating and sugarcraft, so I have included several cakes in this book that can be completed easily, even if you have an eye on the turntable and an ear listening for the baby alarm. There are cake designs in this book that cater for twins and older children, as well as for non-religious celebrations, and a colour change can transform all the cakes to suit boys or girls. You can use either fruit cake or sponge cake as your base, but remember that young children will probably prefer the more subtle taste of sponge cake.

Before starting any of the projects in the book, I would recommend reading the techniques and modelling sections, and don't forget that a very useful size guide can be found in the templates section. If you trace this onto card and cut out the circles, you will be able to check that you are using the right sized ball of paste for the item specified.

Have fun!

Linda Pawsey

Equipment

The following basic equipment is required to produce all the cakes in this book. Where specific cutters, embossers or other equipment are required, these are itemized with the individual cake designs, but you will also find a list opposite of special equipment used in the book.

BASIC EQUIPMENT

- ♥ Large and small non-stick rolling pins and boards
- ♥ Tilting turnable
- ♥ Selection of good-quality paintbrushes
- ♥ Palette knife
- ♥ Craft knife or scalpel and cutting wheel
- ♥ Piping tubes (tips) size 0, 1, 2
- ♥ Scriber
- ♥ Straight edge or icing ruler
- ♥ Tracing paper and card for templates
- ♥ Thin blade scissors
- ♥ Piping bags
- ♥ Edible glue
- ♥ Icing sugar dredger
- ♥ Small dusting bag containing a 50:50 mixture of cornflour and icing sugar
- ♥ Handled smoother
- ♥ Piping gel
- ♥ White vegetable fat
- ♥ Navy and pink food colours
- ♥ Ball modelling tools
- ♥ Celstick and soft pad

Clouds and puffs of smoke are easy to make from thinly rolled white modelling paste using the template on page 104.

Frill the edges of modelling paste using a plastic celstick (see pages 92–3 for full instructions).

The special equipment list details the various specialized items you will require for different projects in the book. Check the individual cake for specific equipment required, and note that there are always alternatives available if you cannot obtain the exact items that I have used. Don't be afraid to adjust the designs to give your own creativity a chance.

Textures

Although there are excellent textured rolling pins available, don't be afraid to experiment with plastic lace. This is widely available and is either sold from a roll, usually 30cm (12in) wide or as doilies.

Use plastic lace to create an interesting texture on your paste.

Templates

The usual method for side and top designs is to use greaseproof paper or parchment. Calculating the measurements for dividing your cake sides or top into quarters, sixths or whatever division you require is a very tedious and laborious task. Nowadays, however, commercial templates are now available that will do the job for you. These are pre-cut and made of plastic so they can be used time and time again instead of starting from scratch each time you make a cake. Measurements and guidance for positioning are already marked so your designs can be drawn and marked in a quarter of the time it would normally take.

SPECIAL EQUIPMENT

- Ring cutters (various sizes)
- Kit-box templates
- Lace cutters
- Assorted stencils
- Leaf and flower cutters
- Plastic lace
- Leaf veiners
- Quilted cutter
- Maidenhair fern cutter
- Embossers
- Styrene flower formers
- Styrene egg
- All-in-one rose cutter
- Silk-effect rolling pin
- Plaque cutter
- Baby's head mould
- Lace leaf cutter
- Curved-blade tool

Cutters come in all the standard shapes and many unusual ones.

Recipes

Madeira sponge (layer) cake

Square tin (pan)		15cm (6in)	18cm (7in)	20cm (8in)	25cm (10in)
Round tin (pan)	**15cm (6in)**	**18cm (7in)**	**20cm (8in)**	**23cm (9in)**	
Self-raising flour	175g (6oz/1$^{1}/_{2}$ cups)	225g (8oz/2 cups)	290g (10oz/2$^{1}/_{2}$ cups)	350g (12oz/3 cups)	500g (1lb 2oz/4$^{1}/_{2}$ cups)
Butter (soft)	120g (4oz/$^{1}/_{2}$ cup)	175g (6oz/$^{3}/_{4}$ cup)	225g (8oz/1 cup)	290g (10oz/1$^{1}/_{4}$ cups)	450g (1lb/2 cups)
Caster (superfine) sugar	120g (4oz/$^{1}/_{2}$ cup)	175g (6oz/$^{3}/_{4}$ cup)	225g (8oz/1 cup)	290g (10oz/1$^{1}/_{4}$ cups)	450g (1lb/2 cups)
Eggs (medium)	2	3	4	5	9
Milk	15ml (1 tbsp)	30ml (2 tbsp)	30ml (2 tbsp)	45ml (3 tbsp)	60ml (4tbsp)
Baking time (approx)	1$^{1}/_{4}$hrs	1$^{1}/_{4}$hrs	1$^{3}/_{4}$hrs	2hrs	2$^{1}/_{4}$hrs

1 Preheat the oven to 160–170°C (325°F/Gas 3). Grease and line the tin (pan).

2 Sift the flour into a bowl, add the soft butter and caster (superfine) sugar and beat until the mixture is pale and smooth. Then add the eggs and milk and beat well, adding more flour if necessary.

3 Spoon the mixture into the tin, then make a dip in the top with the back of a spoon.

4 Bake in the centre of the oven. To test when it is ready, insert a skewer. If it comes out clean, the cake is ready. Leave the cake to stand in the tin for 5 minutes then turn it out onto a wire rack to cool.

Rich fruit cake

Square tin (pan)	12cm (5in)	18cm (7in)	23cm (9in)	28cm (11in)
Round tin (pan)	**15cm (6in)**	**20cm (8in)**	**25cm (10in)**	**30cm (12in)**
Plain (all-purpose) flour	140g (4$^{3}/_{4}$oz/1$^{1}/_{4}$ cups)	230g (8oz/2 cups)	370g (13oz/3$^{1}/_{4}$ cups)	570g (20oz/5 cups)
Muscovado sugar	140g (4$^{3}/_{4}$oz/$^{3}/_{4}$ cup)	230g (8oz/1$^{1}/_{3}$ cups)	370g (13oz/2$^{1}/_{4}$ cups)	570g (20oz/3$^{1}/_{3}$ cups)
Butter/margarine	140g (4$^{3}/_{4}$oz/$^{2}/_{3}$ cup)	230g (8oz/1 cup)	370g (13oz/1$^{2}/_{3}$ cups)	570g (20oz/2$^{1}/_{2}$ cups)
Eggs (beaten)	140g (4$^{3}/_{4}$oz)	230g (8oz)	370g (13oz)	570g (20oz)
Ground almonds	40g (1$^{1}/_{4}$oz/$^{1}/_{3}$ cup)	55g (2oz/$^{1}/_{2}$ cup)	115g (4oz/1 cup)	175g (6oz/1$^{1}/_{2}$ cups)
Currants	280g (10oz/2 cups)	460g (1lb/3 cups)	740g (1lb 9oz/5 cups)	1.14kg (2$^{1}/_{2}$lb/8 cups)
Sultanas (golden raisins)	210g (7$^{1}/_{2}$oz/1$^{1}/_{2}$ cups)	340g (12oz/2$^{1}/_{2}$ cups)	540g (1lb 3oz/3$^{3}/_{4}$ cups)	850g (1lb 15oz/6 cups)
Glacé cherries	40g (1$^{1}/_{2}$oz/$^{1}/_{3}$ cup)	80g (3oz/$^{2}/_{3}$ cup)	115g (4oz/1 cup)	175g (6oz/1$^{1}/_{2}$ cups)
Mixed peel	30g (1oz/$^{1}/_{4}$ cup)	40g (1$^{1}/_{2}$oz/$^{1}/_{3}$ cup)	85g (3oz/$^{3}/_{4}$ cup)	115g (4oz/1 cup)
Mixed spice	2.5ml ($^{1}/_{2}$ tsp)	5ml (1 tsp)	7.5ml (1$^{1}/_{2}$ tsp)	10ml (2 tsp)
Grand Marnier liqueur	45ml (1$^{1}/_{2}$ fl oz)	90ml (3fl oz)	140ml (4$^{1}/_{2}$fl oz)	185ml (6fl oz)
Baking time (approx)	4 hrs	6–7 hrs	8–9 hrs	10–11 hrs

1 Place the dried fruit, peel, cherries and liqueur in a bowl. Cover and leave overnight.

2 Line the cake tin (pan) with greaseproof paper (parchment) and preheat the oven to 150°C (300°F/Gas 2).

3 Cream the butter and sugar together then beat in the eggs. Mix the sifted flour, mixed spice and ground almonds then beat them lightly into the mixture. Add the dried fruit mixture. Stir in a little more flour at this stage if the mixture looks runny.

4 Spoon into the tin and bake in the centre of the oven. After 2 hours, turn the temperature down to 140°C (275°F/Gas 1) for the remainder of the baking time. Insert a skewer and if it comes out clean, the cake is ready. Leave it to cool in the tin.

Royal icing

♥ 2–3 large egg whites
♥ 450g (1lb/4 cups) bridal icing (confectioner's) sugar, sifted

1 Wash and dry all bowls and utensils thoroughly to ensure they are clean and free from grease.

2 Crack the egg whites into a bowl and whisk or beat with a fork until frothy.

3 Add one third of the icing (confectioner's) sugar and mix well.

4 Gradually add the remainder of the icing sugar, beating with a fork or whisk after each addition until soft peaks form in the mixture. It is now ready to use.

Alternative method

If you prefer to use albumen powder instead of egg whites, the proportions are generally as follows:

♥ 12.5g (¹/₂oz/2–3 tsp) albumen powder
♥ 90ml (3fl oz) water
♥ 450g (1lb/4 cups) bridal icing (confectioner's) sugar, sifted

1 Gently whisk the albumen into the water and leave to stand for 30 minutes.

2 Stir the mixture to dissolve any lumps, then strain.

3 Add one third of the icing (confectioner's) sugar and mix well.

4 Gradually add the remainder of the icing sugar, beating with a fork or whisk after each addition until soft peaks form. NOTE: If the icing is not beaten enough, it will be heavy, dull and glossy.

The clouds on Making a Splash, pages 50–3, are made with royal icing using brush embroidery (see page 12).

Royal icing for brush embroidery

♥ 60ml (4 tbsp) soft peak royal icing

♥ 5ml (1 tsp) piping gel

The addition of piping gel to royal icing delays the drying process, allowing you time to paint with it and draw the icing to various shapes without it skinning over too quickly. Stir the piping gel gradually into the royal icing.

Sugarpaste (rolled fondant)

♥ 1 egg white made up from dried egg albumen

♥ 30ml (2 tbsp) liquid glucose

♥ 625g (1lb 5oz/5 cups) icing (confectioner's) sugar

♥ a little white vegetable fat (shortening) if required

1 Put the egg white and liquid glucose into a bowl, using a warm spoon for the liquid glucose.

2 Sift the icing (confectioner's) sugar into the bowl, adding a little at a time and stirring well until the mixture has thickened.

3 Turn out onto a work surface dusted with icing sugar and knead the paste until it is soft, smooth and pliable.

A Gift for Baby, pages 16–18, is covered with white sugarpaste.

If the paste is dry and cracked, fold in a little vegetable fat (shortening) and knead again.

4 Put into a polythene bag, or double wrap the paste in cling film (plastic wrap), and store in an airtight container.

Flower paste (gum paste)

♥ 25ml (5tsp) cold water

♥ 10ml (2tsp) powdered gelatine

♥ 500g (1lb 2oz/3 cups) icing (confectioner's) sugar, sifted

♥ 15ml (3tsp) gum tragacanth

♥ 10ml (2tsp) liquid glucose

♥ 15ml (3tsp) white vegetable fat (shortening)

♥ 1 medium egg white (preferably free-range)

1 Mix the water and the gelatine together in a small heatproof bowl and leave to stand for 30 minutes.

2 Sift the icing (confectioner's) sugar and gum tragacanth into the bowl of a heavy-duty mixer and mix.

3 Place the bowl with the gelatine mixture over a saucepan of hot water and stir until the gelatine has dissolved. Warm a teaspoon in hot water, then measure out the liquid glucose (the heat should help to ease the glucose off the spoon). Add the glucose and white fat to the gelatine mixture and continue to heat until all of the ingredients have melted and are thoroughly mixed together.

4 Add the dissolved gelatine mixture to the icing sugar, along with the egg white. Fit the beater to the machine and turn it on at its lowest speed. Beat until mixed, then increase the speed to maximum until the paste becomes white and stringy.

5 Remove the paste from the bowl and rub a thin layer of white fat over it to prevent the outer part drying out. Place

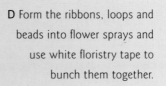

C Attach strips of white paste in diagonal lines round the sides and insert the word 'baby' at evenly spaced intervals.

D Form the ribbons, loops and beads into flower sprays and use white floristry tape to bunch them together.

E Insert a flower pick into the cake top (offset), then insert one of the sprays into the pick and position the other on the board.

Letters

3 Roll out the mid blue modelling paste quite thinly and use an alphabet cutter to cut seven sets of the word 'baby' (see B on page 16).

4 Score the sides of the cake in diagonal lines approximately 7.5cm (3in) to 10cm (4in) apart. The spacing may be more accurate if you make a template before doing this. Cut several long strips of white modelling paste, each 6mm (¹/₄in) wide. Attach these strips along the scored lines on the cake and insert the word 'baby' at regular intervals along each strip (see C).

Ribbons

5 Cut all the ribbons into lengths of 50cm (1²/₃ft). Shred the pale blue floristry ribbon into thin strips. Form the lengths of lustre and silver ribbon into three wired loops (see D).

6 To form the sprays, divide the ribbon loops and beads into two batches, tidying up any frayed or uneven ends of ribbon.

7 Gather up the ribbons and wired beads, arrange in a posy shape and tape together with white floristry tape.

Assembly

8 Insert a flower pick into the top of the cake, near the cake edge. Insert one of the ribbon sprays into the pick (see E).

9 Trim the wires of the second spray and arrange it on the board on the opposite side of the cake.

The elegant white storks on this cake are a stylish version of a very popular decorative theme. Although the modelling requires care and patience, I hope you will feel that these lovely birds are worth the time they take to make.

Elegant Storks

CAKE AND DECORATION

- 1.5kg (3¹/4lb) sugarpaste (rolled fondant)
- 25cm (10in) and 15cm (6in) scalloped oval cakes
- apricot glaze or clear alcohol (gin or vodka)
- 1.25kg (2³/4lb) almond paste
- 115g (4oz) royal icing
- 1.5m (5ft) narrow green ribbon
- edible glue
- 225g (8oz) white modelling paste
- 15g (¹/2oz) each of pale pink and pale green flower paste (gum paste)
- pastel lustre colour

SPECIAL EQUIPMENT

- 30cm (12in) scalloped oval cake board
- silk-effect rolling pin (OP)
- 15cm (6in) thin cake card
- modelling size guide (see page 107)
- one length of 18 gauge wire
- small all-in-one rose cutter (OP)
- miniature vine leaf cutter (KB)

Preparing the cakes and boards

1 To cover the large cake board, roll out a 7.5cm (3in) long strip of white sugarpaste (rolled fondant). Roll the paste with the textured rolling pin and attach around the cake board (see A). Set aside to dry. Attach the small cake to a thin cake card exactly the same size as the cake, and sit this on a larger board to minimize handling.

2 Brush both the cakes with apricot glaze or alcohol (gin or vodka), then cover with almond paste. Leave to dry. Brush with alcohol, then cover with white sugarpaste. Leave to dry for at least 24 hours. Attach the larger cake to the covered board with a little royal icing. Attach the small cake on top in an off-set position (see B). Attach a narrow green ribbon round the base of both cakes with edible glue.

A Roll the paste with a textured rolling pin and attach it to the large cake board then leave it to dry.

B Place the small cake on top of the large one and attach narrow green ribbon around the base of each cake.

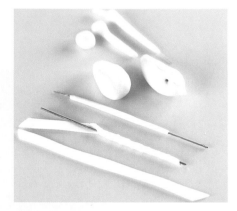

C Mould the body, legs, neck and head of the stork and leave them aside to dry completely.

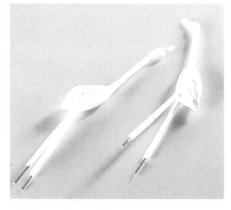

D Use a little royal icing to attach the legs and neck to the body. Blend the icing in with a damp paintbrush.

E Attach the finished storks to the cake. One stands on the top cake and the other on the bottom one.

Stork

3 Roll a ball of white modelling paste to a size 26. Form the ball into a cone approximately 5cm (2in) long. Cut the tapered end of the cone into three to form a tail. Underneath the body, form two holes for the leg sockets, then form one at the top for the neck.

4 For the legs, cut two pieces of 18 gauge wire into 10cm (4in) lengths. Now roll out some white modelling paste and cut two strips 10cm (4in) long and 3mm (1/8in) wide. Paint edible glue onto the strip and wrap this around the wire, leaving 2cm (3/4in) of exposed wire; repeat to complete the other leg (see C).

5 For the neck, use a large pea-sized ball of modelling paste. Roll the paste into a sausage shape until it is 5cm (2in) long, leaving a ball shape at one end to form the head. At the front of the head, pinch a tiny section of paste and roll gently to form a narrow beak. Insert a white 18 gauge wire 5cm (2in) long up into the neck leaving a small amount protruding from the base. Set all the pieces aside to dry.

6 To assemble the bird, pipe a small amount of royal icing into the leg sockets and insert the legs. Blend in the royal icing by brushing with a damp paintbrush. Attach the neck to the body the same way (see D). The finished bird should be approximately 15cm (6in) tall. Make the second stork in the same way, but with the head bent into a slightly different position (see E). Allow the birds to dry for at least 3 days before attaching them to the cake.

F Using either an all-in-one rose cutter or a blossom cutter, make seven roses out of pale pink modelling paste.

G Use a silk-effect rolling pin to texture the white modelling paste used to make the drape, forming gentle folds.

H Attach the drape, then insert the roses and vine leaves into the scallops around the top edges of the cake.

Miniature roses

7 Seven miniature roses are required for this cake. Using the pale pink flower paste, form seven tiny cone shapes on wires for the centres of the roses. Leave to dry for a few hours.

8 Using a 2.5cm (1in) blossom or all-in-one rose cutter, cut two blossoms. Take one of the blossoms, and ball around the edges to soften. Lightly brush some glue onto one of the petals and thread the cone through the centre, wrapping the glued petal around the cone (see F). Glue and wrap two alternate petals around the cone and then the remaining two should overlap.

9 Ball the edges of the second blossom, glue and attach to the underside of the flower, curving the petals back slightly. Make the other roses and, when the outer petals are dry, gently slide each rose off the wire and set aside to dry.

Vine leaves

10 Using the pale green flower paste, roll out and cut 14 miniature vine leaves. On a soft pad, ball the edges and fold each leaf to form a centre vein, then allow to dry.

Making the drape

11 Roll out 100g (3 1/2oz) of white modelling paste and cut a very large leaf shape with a point at both ends. Using the silk-effect rolling pin, texture the paste. Turn the paste over and fold over the edges to form a hem. Turn the paste back onto the right side and gently gather up sections to form gentle folds (see G).

12 Whilst still soft, attach the paste to the small cake, draping it onto the larger cake. When you are happy with the position of the drape, attach with edible glue. When the drape has dried completely, paint with lustre colour.

Attaching the flowers and leaves

13 Using a skewer or celstick, make a hole at the top edge of the cake in each of the scallops on both cakes. Pipe a small quantity of royal icing into each hole and gently insert a miniature rose.

14 Attach a vine leaf to either side of the rose with royal icing and pipe three small dots on the outside edge of each leaf (see H).

Attaching the storks

15 To hold the storks, place a ball of paste under the drape at both ends, ensuring that they cannot be seen. Make two holes for each stork, using the legs of each to impress the drape. Pipe a small amount of royal icing into each of the holes. Insert the storks, making sure that the wires stay only in the paste and do not pierce the cake (see I).

16 Using a small calyx cutter or a similar cutter, cut and trim four feet. Brush with glue and attach to the bottom of the legs (see J).

17 To finish the cake, brush the textured paste on the board with the same lustre colour that was used for the drape (see K). NOTE: Check that it is edible – some colours are not.

I When inserting the storks' legs into the paste, be sure that the wires do not penetrate the cake as well.

J Cut and trim the feet on each stork, then use edible glue to attach them to the drape at the base of the legs.

K Brush the cake board with lustre colour, to give a beautiful frosted finish to the textured board.

This delightful two-tier stacked cake would be ideal for a christening or naming ceremony that will be attended by older children. You could make a keepsake teddy for each of the baby's siblings so they don't feel left out.

Teddies' Presents

CAKE AND DECORATION

- ♥ 1.25kg (2^{1}/2lb) ivory sugarpaste (rolled fondant)
- ♥ apricot glaze or clear alcohol (gin or vodka)
- ♥ 900g (2lb) almond paste
- ♥ 25cm (10in) and 15cm (6in) oval cakes
- ♥ 50g (2oz) royal icing
- ♥ 15g (^{1}/2oz) each of lilac, lemon, pink and green modelling paste
- ♥ 50g (2oz) white modelling paste
- ♥ 225g (8oz) dark cream modelling paste
- ♥ 25g (1oz) dark brown modelling paste
- ♥ edible glue
- ♥ dark brown food colouring
- ♥ 2m (6^{1}/2ft) 1cm (^{1}/2in) wide pink ribbon

SPECIAL EQUIPMENT

- ♥ 30cm (1ft) long octagonal cake board
- ♥ 15cm (6in) thin cake card
- ♥ building blocks cutters (PC from nursery set)

Preparing the cakes and board

1 Cover the cake board with ivory sugarpaste (rolled fondant), using a smoother to ensure an even surface finish. Set aside to dry.

2 Brush the cakes with apricot glaze or alcohol (gin or vodka), whichever you prefer, and cover with almond paste. Leave to dry. Brush the almond paste with alcohol, then cover with ivory sugarpaste. Allow to dry for at least 24 hours.

3 Attach the larger cake to the long octagonal board with a little royal icing, positioning it in the centre of the board. Attach the smaller cake to a cake card the same size as the cake and position it on top of the large cake.

A Make the presents from modelling paste in different colours and sizes, varying the look of the ribbons and bows tied around them.

B Mould the bears' bodies, arms and legs in dark cream modelling paste. There are three different sizes of bear – large, medium and baby.

C Use a ball shape for the head and pinch it to form a snout and neck, then mark the bear's features.

D Attach the bears' limbs to the bodies. Circles of paste are added to make a jumper and collar.

E Dress the bears in jackets, polo necks or bows, choosing colours to complement the cake design.

Presents

4 Using the lilac, lemon, pink and green modelling paste, mould different-sized cubes of paste (see A on page 24). Score the edges to look like folded paper. For the ribbons and bows, roll out white modelling paste very thinly and cut narrow strips. Wrap these around the presents and attach them with edible glue. Attach small loops and tails to the tops of the presents. Pushing a tiny amount of paste through a tea strainer gives a dainty bow.

Teddies

5 See the detailed instructions for the moulding and shaping of a baby's body, limbs and head given on pages 66–8. With dark cream modelling paste, mould four different-sized teddies. The largest bear has a 50g (2oz) body; mould this piece into a cone shape approximately 7.5cm (3in) long. Squeeze gently on either side of the fat end of the cone to form sockets for the legs. Make holes in these sockets, then make two more holes on either side of the top of the cone for the arms and one on the top for the neck. To give the impression of hair, score the paste with a curved blade modelling tool or craft knife. Make two smaller bodies using 15g (¹/₂oz) pieces of paste then make a tiny body for the baby bear with a 7.5g (¹/₄oz) piece.

6 To make the legs and arms for the large bear, use a 15g (¹/₂oz) ball of paste for each limb (see B on page 24). For the two medium-sized bears, make limbs from 7.5g (¹/₄oz) balls of paste and make the baby's limbs

from balls of paste that are half as small again.
NOTE: Practise modelling for realistic results.

Head

7 For the large bear, roll a 25g (1oz) piece of
paste into a ball shape. Gently pinch a snout
and a neck from the soft paste. Mark the
features with a craft knife and skewer (see C).
For the medium-sized bear, use a 15g (1/2oz)
ball of paste and for the baby, a 7.5g (1/4oz) ball.
NOTE: A piece of uncooked spaghetti can be
inserted into the neck for added strength.

Assembly

8 When all the body parts are dry, attach the
arms and legs to each of the bodies with
softened modelling paste. Make the eyes and
noses from tiny balls of dark brown modelling
paste. Paint the features with dark brown
food colouring, using a good-quality fine brush
for a neat finish. Attach each bear's head
to its body with softened modelling paste.

9 Add clothing by attaching a circle of paste
over the top of the body and arms (see D).
Make collars and polo necks from a ball or circle
of paste (see E). For the baby teddy bear, add a
small pink bow and a dummy (see F and G).

Decorating the sides

10 Using the cutter, cut out building blocks.
Attach the white ribbon to the base of the cake
then stick the building blocks onto the ribbon
(see H). Position the large teddy holding the
baby bear on the small cake and arrange the
gifts and other bears around the base.

F Use thin strips of pink
modelling paste to make a
bow and a dummy for the
baby bear.

G Wrap the bow round the
baby bear's head and place the
dummy in its mouth. Position
in the mother bear's arms.

H Wrap the white ribbon
around the cake board and
stick the ivory paste building
blocks around the cake.

I imagine these lovely little angels are just how we thought our own children would be. It is a good idea to model these cherubs well in advance of the celebration day, so that they will be thoroughly dried and easier to handle when you are preparing the cake.

Little Angels

CAKE AND DECORATION

300g (10¹/₂oz) blue sugarpaste (rolled fondant)

25cm (10in) and 10cm (4in) round cakes

apricot glaze or clear alcohol (gin or vodka)

1.13kg (2¹/₂lb) almond paste

a little royal icing

1kg (2¹/₄lb) white sugarpaste

2m (6¹/₂ft) wide pearlescent floristry ribbon

piping gel

25g (1oz) pale green modelling paste

15g (¹/₂oz) each of white and pale yellow modelling paste

225g (8oz) flesh modelling paste

25g (1oz) white flower paste (gum paste)

edible glue

food colouring

lustre colour

A Cut the cloud shapes from pearlescent floristry ribbon, to give a shimmer to the cake sides.

B Using royal icing, pipe three groups of little birds in flight, spacing them evenly round the sides of the cake.

SPECIAL EQUIPMENT

35cm (14in) round board and 10cm (4in) cake card

piping bag with no. 1 tube (tip)

grape mould (SC) and baby head mould (HP)

modelling size guide (see page 107)

template (see page 102)

butterfly cutter (KB)

one length of silver floristry wire

Preparing the cake and board

1 Cover the cake board with blue sugarpaste (rolled fondant) using a smoother to ensure an even finish. Set aside to dry.

2 Brush the cakes with apricot glaze or alcohol (gin or vodka). Attach the small cake to the cake card and cover both cakes with almond paste. Leave to dry. Brush with

C Form ribbons and bows from white modelling paste and attach them between the bunches of green grapes.

D There are three angels. Make cones for their bodies and make holes to form sockets for the arms, legs and neck.

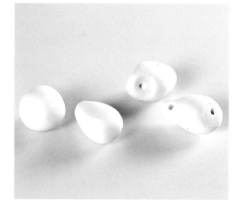

E Remember to create both left and right sets of arms and legs and mark little fingers and toes.

alcohol, then cover the large cake with white sugarpaste and the smaller one with blue. (Sit the small cake and card onto a larger board to minimize handling.) Leave to dry for 24 hours. Attach the large cake to the centre of the board with a little royal icing. Attach the small cake to the large cake in an off-centre position.

Side decoration

3 Cut two lengths of pearlescent floristry ribbon to fit the circumference of the cake. Now cut cloud shapes along the length of the ribbon (see A on page 28).

4 Attach the ribbon clouds around the bottom edge of each cake with piping gel. With a small amount of soft peak royal icing in a bag with a no. I tube (tip), pipe groups of three tiny birds on the sides of the cakes (see B on page 28).

5 Using a small quantity of pale green modelling paste and a grape mould, press out several tiny bunches of grapes. Attach these with edible glue in a curve around one side of each of the cakes.

6 Cut thin strips of white modelling paste to form ribbons and bows and attach these in between the bunches of grapes (see C).

Angels

7 See the instructions on Modelling Babies, pages 66–8, for more information. You will need to make three complete angels, one sitting, one lying down and one standing. Form a size 22 ball of flesh-coloured modelling paste into a

cone 3.5cm (1¹/₂in) long. Pinch the fat end of the cone with finger and thumb to form sockets for the legs. With a skewer or celstick, make a hole at the top of the thin end of the cone to form a neck socket, then make holes for arm and leg sockets (see D).

8 For the legs, roll a sausage 3.5cm (1¹/₂in) long with a size 16 ball of paste. Form a knee by bending the sausage in the middle and roll the shape a little more thinly at one end so that it tapers towards the ankle. Gently squeeze the bulb of paste to form a foot above the ankle. Bend this section over slightly and cut toes.

9 For the arms, form a size 15 ball of paste into a sausage 3.5cm (1¹/₂in) long. Roll to narrow the paste slightly at one end to form the wrist. Flatten the end to make an oval shape to form the hand, and cut for the fingers. Repeat, remembering to form right and left arms (see E).

10 For the heads, use a baby head mould and a size 26 ball of flesh-coloured paste (see F). Set aside to dry for at least 48 hours. With pale yellow modelling paste, add a ball of paste to the back of each head and ease forward to mould the hair around the face. Paint the faces with edible food colour and a fine paintbrush.

11 For the wings, roll out a small amount of white flower paste (gum paste) and cut four sets of wings using a butterfly cutter (as these are fragile, cut spares). Frill the edges of the wings with a skewer or celstick. Bend and dry over foam. Brush with lustre colour (see G).

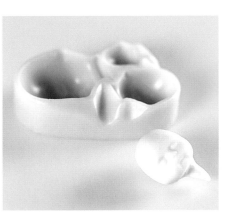

F Use a baby head mould to form the heads then let them dry for at least 48 hours before painting the faces.

G Use a butterfly cutter to make the wings then frill the edges with a celstick. Brush them with lustre colour.

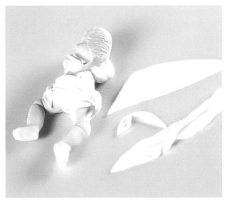

H Make nappies from white flower paste then lie the babies face down to attach the wings with royal icing.

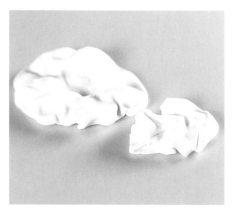

I Make four clouds with thinly rolled modelling paste, so that they look soft and fluffy when the paste is folded.

J Secure the babies to the clouds with royal icing, arranging the standing babies against the side of the cake.

K Flags can be cut from either flower paste or paper. Don't forget you can personalize your message.

12 To assemble the angels, pipe soft peak royal icing into the sockets of the body and attach the arms, legs and heads. Lay out on foam and allow to dry at least overnight.

13 To make the nappies, cut an elongated leaf shape from thinly rolled flower paste, and attach one nappy to each baby with edible glue. Gather up the paste so that it looks a bit like a loin cloth. To form the knots, add tiny tails to each side of the nappy. At this stage, carefully attach one set of wings to the back of each baby with a little royal icing. Lie the babies on their fronts to allow the wings to set in position (see H on page 31).

Clouds and banners

14 To make the clouds, fold thin modelling paste into a drape similar to that used on Elegant Storks (see page 24). Make four clouds (see I). Whilst still soft, attach the clouds to the cakes and position the babies in them, attaching them securely with royal icing.
NOTE: It is best to lean the standing babies against the sides of the cake for support (see J).

15 To make the banners, roll out and cut flags (using the template on page 102) from white flower paste (gum paste), and allow them to dry (see K). Write greetings to the new baby then attach them securely to pieces of wire and position them so that they rest on the cake and lean against the angels' hands. (Paper flags can be used as an alternative to paste.)
NOTE: Make sure that the wires are removed before the cake is served.

A very easy cake to make, that uses soft pastel colours. Your chosen name or greeting can be incorporated into the coloured squares on the top or sides. Additional letters and hearts could be used to decorate the table.

Alphabet Heart

CAKE AND DECORATION

- ♥ 1kg (2¼lb) ivory sugarpaste (rolled fondant)
- ♥ 25cm (10in) heart-shaped cake
- ♥ apricot glaze or clear alcohol (gin or vodka)
- ♥ 900g (2lb) almond paste
- ♥ a little royal icing
- ♥ 25g (1oz) each of pale lilac, pale green, pale yellow and pale blue modelling paste
- ♥ edible glue
- ♥ 1m (3ft) ivory ribbon

SPECIAL EQUIPMENT

- ♥ 33cm (13in) heart-shaped cake board
- ♥ alphabet cutter (FMM)
- ♥ small square cutters (FMM)

Preparing the cake and board

1 Cover the cake board with ivory sugarpaste (rolled fondant) using a smoother to ensure an even surface finish. Set aside to dry. Brush the cake with apricot glaze or alcohol (gin or vodka), whichever you prefer, and cover with almond paste. Leave to dry. Brush the almond paste with alcohol, then cover with ivory sugarpaste. Leave to dry for at least 24 hours. Attach the cake to the board with a little royal icing, positioning it in the centre of the board.

Hearts

2 Roll out some pale lilac-coloured modelling paste and cut out several small hearts. Repeat to cut out several in the pale green and pale yellow paste (see A).

A Using a heart-shaped cutter, cut out lots of hearts in pale lilac, pale green and pale yellow modelling paste.

B Cut out several letters with the alphabet cutter, remembering that you will need extra letters for the name on the top of the cake.

C Cut out pastel squares: the number required depends on the number of letters in the name on top of the cake.

D Attach the letters to the centres of the pastel squares, making sure that the bases of the letters are properly aligned.

E Cut a right-angle into each of the squares at the side so that they fit together neatly.

Letters

3 Roll out the blue modelling paste and cut several letters of the alphabet, using alphabet cutters. In addition to these letters, cut out the letters of the name you want to feature on the top of the cake (see B on page 33).

Coloured squares

4 Using each of the pastel colours in turn, cut out in modelling paste the following squares using card templates or square cutters: three lilac, 3.5cm (1½in); six yellow, 2.5cm (1in); and six green, 2.5cm (1in) (see C). NOTE: The number of coloured squares required for the top of the cake will depend on the name displayed. If the name has an even number of letters, arrange the squares in a curve, rather than an inverted 'V' shape as shown.

5 While the squares are still slightly soft, attach the letters to the centres using a small amount of edible glue (see D).

6 Cut tiny right-angles out of the corners of some of the squares so that they slot together (see E). When all the letters have been attached to the squares, arrange them neatly and attach to the sides of the cake. Ensure that the backs of the squares are glued all over so that all the points of the squares make contact with the cake. Follow the same procedure for the baby's name or any greeting you want to include on the top of the cake.

7 Attach the ivory ribbon around the edge of the cake board with glue or double-sided tape.

A colourful cut-out teddy holding strings of pretty balloons provides this royal-iced oval cake with a cheerful decorative motif. It will make a striking centrepiece for your christening celebration table and is equally suitable for boys or girls.

Up, Up and Away Teddy

CAKE AND DECORATION

- 1kg (2¹/4lb) soft peak royal icing
- 25cm (10in) oval cake
- apricot glaze or clear alcohol (gin or vodka)
- 900g (2lb) almond paste
- 25g (1oz) dark cream modelling paste
- 25g (1oz) modelling paste in white and three pastel colours
- edible glue
- 1m (3ft) 5cm (2in) wide blue tulle ribbon
- dark brown food colouring
- 1m (3ft) 1cm (¹/2in) wide blue ribbon

SPECIAL EQUIPMENT

- 33cm (13in) oval cake board
- templates (see page 100)
- craft knife or cutting wheel (PME)
- tracing wheel (PME)
- large and small rose petal cutter (OP)

A Use the templates to cut out the different parts of the teddy bear from dark cream modelling paste.

B Use a large petal cutter to cut out balloons from the pastel or marbled modelling paste.

Preparing the cake and board

1 Cover the cake board with white royal icing or white sugarpaste (rolled fondant). Set aside to dry. Brush the cake with apricot glaze or alcohol (gin or vodka) and cover the sides and top separately with almond paste. Allow to dry overnight. Using soft peak royal icing, coat the cake at least three times to ensure a good finish. Allow each coat to dry for several hours before applying the next. Attach the cake to the board with a little royal icing, positioning it in the centre.

Cut out teddy

2 Trace and cut out the teddy bear sections using the template on page 100. Roll out the dark cream modelling paste thinly, and cut out all the sections of the teddy bear. To

ensure a clean cut, use a craft knife with a new blade or a cutting wheel (see A on page 36). Set aside the sections to dry thoroughly on foam.

Balloons

3 Using the pastel coloured modelling paste, roll out and cut several balloons using a large rose petal cutter. Marbled balloons can be made by combining two colours of paste and folding them together before rolling out (see B on page 36). Set the balloons aside to dry.

NOTE: The number of balloons required will depend on whether or not you want to incorporate the child's name.

C A small petal cutter is used for the balloons that decorate the sides. The balloon strings sit on top of the ribbon.

4 Attach the blue tulle ribbon round the side of the cake with piping gel, and fix small white balloons in groups of three onto the ribbon. With royal icing, pipe white strings leading from each of the balloons (see C).

D Attach the bear's body to the top of the cake with royal icing and position the feet on top, overlapping the body.

Assembling teddy

5 Attach the body and feet of the teddy bear to the top of the cake with soft peak royal icing. The feet should overlap the body (see D).

6 Using soft peak royal icing, attach the balloons around the top edge of the cake, letting them protrude over the edge.

E Attach balloon strings with one end touching the base of a balloon and the other lying under the bear's hand.

7 With dark cream modelling paste, cut a very thin string for each balloon, varying the lengths. Attach one end to the base of each balloon and position the strings so that they will sit underneath the teddy's paw (see E). Using the matching colour paste, make and attach a tiny

ball to the base of each balloon to represent the knot. Now attach paws on top of the strings.

8 Colour a large pea-sized ball of cream modelling paste dark brown, and mould two small ovals for the eyes, and one larger for the nose. Attach the muzzle to the head with edible glue then position the eyes above the muzzle and the nose on top of it (see F).

9 Place three small pieces of modelling paste on the cake just above the body and sit the bear's head on top (see G).

Finishing touches

10 Pipe the word 'Baby' (or your baby's name, or the greeting of your choice) on the balloons, in either the same colour as each balloon or a contrasting shade (see H).

11 Attach the thin blue ribbon around the edge of the cake board with a little glue or double-sided tape,

Variations

To adjust this cake design for twins, reduce the size of the teddy sections using a photocopier and make two smaller bears that can sit side by side on top of the cake. The two groups of balloons can be used for two separate names. If the cake is for a boy and a girl, you could make one bunch of balloons pink and one blue (or other colours of your choice). Don't forget to change the ribbon around the cake to white or a neutral colour if you are using different colours for the balloons.

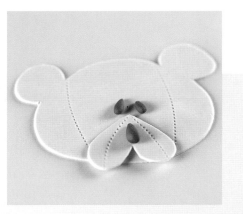

F Make a nose and eyes from dark brown paste. Attach the nose to the muzzle and the eyes just above on the face.

G The bear's head should sit slightly on top of its body. Attach the head with small pieces of modelling paste.

H Pipe the greeting of your choice onto the balloons. It could be the baby's name, a greeting, or the word 'baby'.

Modelling a Crib

FOR THE CRIB

- 225g (8oz) firm white modelling paste, made from 75% flower paste (gum paste) and 25% sugarpaste (rolled fondant)
- edible glue
- royal icing

SPECIAL EQUIPMENT

- piece of foam
- oval template (see page 102)
- thin card
- piece of plastic lace

Preparing the crib

1 Cut a piece of foam into an oval shape – this will act as a support. Use the oval template on page 102 or draw around an oval cutter (see A). Now cut a piece of card that is slightly longer than the circumference of the oval. Wrap the card around the oval shape and join the ends together with masking tape. Two templates are required for the side.

2 Using the second template, roll and cut a strip of firm white modelling paste and fit this around the oval, overlapping the ends slightly (see B). Glue the ends together with edible glue. Allow to dry for at least 24 hours.

3 Using the same size template, roll, cut and pleat several sections of modelling paste and attach them with glue to the dried sides of the crib (see C). (See pages 86–7 for instructions on pleating.)

Canopy

4 Cut another template for the canopy. The one used here is 10cm (4in) tall and 15cm (6in) wide. Roll, cut and pleat two canopy sections (see D).

A Cut an oval piece of foam to act as a support while the crib is drying.

B Roll and cut a strip of modelling paste to fit around the oval card.

C Pleat and emboss sections and attach them to the side of the crib.

D Roll, cut and pleat two canopy sections plus a rolled strip for the top.

E When dry, pipe royal icing onto the top of the join to strengthen it.

F Attach the canopy to the base using supports until it is dry.

This beautiful crib is displayed on a petal-shaped cake on page 77.

G Make a frilled strip of paste and a pink bow for the top of the canopy.

H Stick the frill and bow to the top of the canopy while still soft.

I The baby and cover are attached with a little royal icing when the crib has dried completely.

Allow to dry on foam for at least 3 days. When completely dry, roll a thin sausage of paste the width of the finished sections. This will bind the sections together.

5 Stand the canopy sections upright, being very careful not to break them (see E on page 41). Pipe royal icing on either side of the strip and join the two pieces at the top. The opening at the bottom of the canopy should fit exactly over the crib base. Support the canopy with foam so that it stays open in exactly the right position. After 24 hours, pipe more royal icing onto the top of the joined pieces to give added strength.

6 Attach the canopy to the base with royal icing, using supports to keep it in position (see F on page 41). A further frilled canopy section is added while it is still soft, to fill in the gap at the back of the canopy.

7 Roll, cut and frill a narrow strip that will neatly cover the join at the top of the canopy (see G). Make a small pink bow.

8 While still soft, attach the frilled strip to the top of the canopy with more royal icing. Fold it over so that it sits neatly on either side of the canopy. Attach the bow to the front of the top of the canopy (see H). Instructions for making and attaching the baby's head, pillow and cover are given on pages 78–9 in Draped Lace Crib (see I).

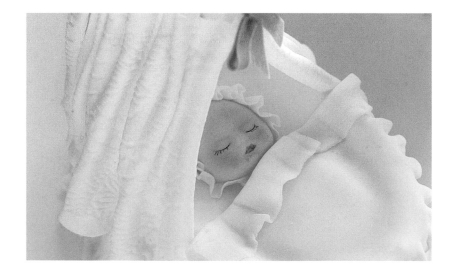

A delightful cake that is simple to make since it does not take long to create the pretty decorations. Blossom cutters are used for the tiny pink flowers and a quilted cutter creates the pattern on the bib.

Bib and Blossoms

CAKE AND DECORATION

- ♥ 1.4kg (3lb) white sugarpaste (rolled fondant)
- ♥ 20cm (8in) round cake
- ♥ apricot glaze or clear alcohol (gin or vodka)
- ♥ 1.1kg (2¹/₂lb) almond paste
- ♥ a little royal icing
- ♥ 1m (3ft) 4cm (1¹/₂in) wide white satin ribbon
- ♥ edible glue
- ♥ 1m (3ft) 1cm (¹/₂in) wide white ribbon
- ♥ 50g (2oz) pink modelling paste
- ♥ 15g (¹/₂oz) white modelling paste
- ♥ 15ml (1 tbsp) dark green royal icing

SPECIAL EQUIPMENT

- ♥ 28cm (11in) round cake board
- ♥ quilted cutter (PC)
- ♥ tiny blossom cutter (FMM)
- ♥ no. 0 piping tube (tip)

Preparing the cake and board

1 Cover the cake board with white sugarpaste (rolled fondant), using a smoother to ensure an even surface finish. Set aside to dry.

2 Brush the cake with apricot glaze or alcohol (gin or vodka), whichever you prefer, and cover with almond paste. Leave to dry. Brush the almond paste with alcohol, then cover with white sugarpaste. Leave to dry for at least 24 hours. Attach the cake to the board with a little royal icing, positioning it in the centre. Fix the satin ribbon around the base of the cake with edible glue. Above the ribbon make holes at intervals of approximately 5–8cm (2–3in) around the cake, ready to hold the blossoms (see A). The narrower white ribbon should be glued around the cake board.

A Attach the satin ribbon round the cake then make little holes above it at regular intervals. These will hold the blossoms.

B Make as many blossoms as you like. There are 30 on the cake pictured but you might like to add more.

Blossoms

3 Roll out a little pink modelling paste and cut 30 tiny blossoms with the tiny blossom cutter (see B on page 43). Set them aside to dry.

Bib

4 Roll out 25g (1oz) pink modelling paste and use a quilted embossing cutter to impress the paste and give a quilted finish. Cut a 7.5cm (3in) circle. Use the same cutter to cut a small piece from the top of the bib (see C).

C Cut out the bib and emboss it with a quilted cutter. Frill the edges with a celstick and make little stitch marks.

5 Immediately after cutting, frill the edge of the bib by rolling a celstick firmly backwards and forwards on the edge. Mark the bib to form stiches. With a little royal icing, attach the bib to the cake (slightly off centre). Gently raise the top of the bib to give a little movement and support it with a little piece of foam until dry.

D Arrange the bib on top of the cake, attach the ribbons and decorate them with some little blossoms.

6 For the ribbons of the bib, cut two strips of white modelling paste 15cm (6in) long and 6mm (1/4in) inch wide. While they are still pliable, attach these to the bib with edible glue and fix them to the cake in a curve (see D).

7 Pipe tiny dots of royal icing at intervals along the ribbons and attach blossoms. With a little dark green royal icing and the no.0 piping tube (tip), pipe dots in each blossom centre.

E Press blossoms around the cake sides, mark the centres with dark green icing then pipe white bulbs in between.

Cake sides

8 Pipe a small amount of royal icing into the holes around the sides and gently press a dried pink blossom into each. With white royal icing, pipe a series of large and small bulbs between each of the blossoms (see E).

All babies love bathtime (we hope!). This easy-to-make duckling certainly looks as though he's enjoying his soak. Lots of overlapping circles form a simple but effective collar on this royal-iced cake, like bubbles that have spilled over from the bath.

Duck's Bathtime

CAKE AND DECORATION

- ♥ 1kg (2¼lb) soft peak royal icing
- ♥ 25cm (10in) round cake
- ♥ 900g (2lb) almond paste
- ♥ apricot glaze
- ♥ 75g (3oz) firm white modelling paste
- ♥ edible glue
- ♥ 25g (1oz) pale yellow modelling paste
- ♥ orange food colouring
- ♥ 15g (½oz) orange modelling paste
- ♥ 25g (1oz) white sugarpaste (rolled fondant)
- ♥ pastel lustre colour

SPECIAL EQUIPMENT

- ♥ 33cm (13in) round cake board
- ♥ template (see page 102)
- ♥ modelling size guide (see page 107)
- ♥ curved tool
- ♥ 4 round cutters, up to 5cm (2in) diameter (KB)

A Use templates to cut out the sloping sides and oval base of the duck's bathtub from white modelling paste.

B Make the duck's head from a ball of pale yellow modelling paste. Pinch a beak and neck, then mark the eyelids.

Preparing the cake

1 Brush the cake with apricot glaze and cover the sides and top separately with almond paste. Leave to dry overnight. Using soft peak royal icing, coat the cake at least three times to ensure a good finish. Allow each coat to dry for several hours. Attach the cake to the board with a little royal icing, positioning it in the centre.

Bath

2 Roll out the white modelling paste and cut a strip for the bath sides (see template on page 102). Cut an oval for the base of the bath 5mm (¼in) thick (see A). With edible glue, attach the side strip around the oval shape joining the ends and where the

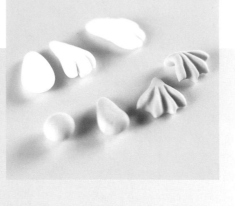

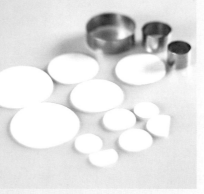

C Mould the wings and feet. Mark feathers on the wings and make indentations for the webbed feet.

D Use different sizes of ring cutter to make the flat bubbles. You will need around 25 of each size.

E Stick the bubbles around the bottom edge of the cake, letting some curve over onto the cake board.

strip meets the oval base. While still soft, gently turn the top edge of the strip outwards to form a lip. Set aside to dry for 24 hours.

Duck

3 With pale yellow modelling paste, form a size 24 ball shape. Pinch one side of the ball to form a beak. Also pinch a small piece of paste to form a neck (see B on page 46). Mark eyelid shapes on the duck's head with a drinking straw so that it looks as if he is sleeping, then mark the feathers with a curved tool. When the head is completely dry, paint the beak with orange food colouring.

4 For the wings, roll two size 16 balls of pale yellow modelling paste into cones. Flatten the fat ends and score with a palette knife to mark feathers, ensuring that you make a right and a left (see C). Curve the wings so that they will sit over the edge of the bath. Set aside to dry.

5 For the feet, use orange modelling paste to form two cones from size 13 balls of paste, and flatten the thick ends. Press the end of a narrow paintbrush or celstick onto the paste in three places to form the webbed feet (see C). Cut out semi-circles between the ridges to complete.

Bubbles

6 Using four different size ring cutters, the largest 5cm (2in), cut circles from firm white modelling paste, ensuring there are enough to go around the top and bottom edge of the cake with a few left to sit on top (see D). Approximately 25 circles of each size will be

plenty. Set aside to dry for at least 24 hours. When dry, brush some of the bubbles with lustre colour to give them a pearly sheen.

7 Attach bubbles around the bottom of the cake and board with soft peak royal icing, letting them curve onto the board (see E).

8 Attach bubbles around the top edge of the cake in the same way, but position some so that they overlap others (see F).

Assembly

9 Place a flattened piece of sugarpaste (rolled fondant) in the bottom of the bath for the duck's body. With royal icing, attach the head, wings and feet (see G).

10 Finally, fill the bath with bubbles. You can do this in one of two ways, either by piping large bulbs of royal icing or by making balls of modelling paste. When the bath is full, adjust the position of the duck's head and feet in the bubbles so it looks as if it is relaxing (see H).

Variation

Although I have used a duck sitting in the bath on this cake, it would work equally well with either an elephant or a rabbit. For an elephant, make a head and four feet, following the instructions in Jumbo Junior's Nap on page 75, and position it in a similar fashion to the duck before adding the bubbles. For a rabbit, follow the instructions given in Twins' Slumber on page 87. Alternatively, model a baby to go in the bath; see pages 66–8.

F Overlap the bubbles around the top edges of the cake, alternating the sizes for a random-looking effect.

G Position a piece of sugarpaste in the bath for the duck's body and attach the head, wings and feet.

H Fill the bath with bubbles! You can make these from balls of modelling paste or by piping bulbs of royal icing.

A plaster wedding cake pillar makes the ideal column for the font for these sweet little modelled bluebirds. Piping gel is used for the water. This is a perfect celebration cake for the christening of a baby boy.

Making a Splash

CAKE AND DECORATION

1.25kg (2¹/₂lb) white sugarpaste (rolled fondant)
25cm (10in) round cake
apricot glaze or clear alcohol (gin or vodka)
900g (2lb) almond paste
50g (2oz) white modelling paste (gum paste)
115g (4oz) royal icing
edible glue
blue, black and orange food colourings
piping gel
1m (3ft) 1cm (¹/₂in) wide blue ribbon
1m (3ft) narrow white ribbon

SPECIAL EQUIPMENT

33cm (13in) round cake board
white plaster pillar
templates (see page 102)
modelling size guide (see page 107)
nos. 1 and 2 piping tubes (tips)

Preparing the cake and board

1 Cover the cake board with white sugarpaste (rolled fondant) using a smoother to ensure an even surface finish. Set aside to dry. Brush the cake with apricot glaze or alcohol (gin or vodka), whichever you prefer, and cover with almond paste. Leave to dry. Brush with alcohol, then cover with white sugarpaste. Leave to dry for at least 24 hours. Attach to the centre of the board with a little royal icing.

Font

2 Roll out some white modelling paste approximately 3mm (¹/₈in) thick and cut out two circles 5cm (2in) wide and two circles 3.5cm (1¹/₂in) wide. Place a small and large circle into a curved former to make the bowl of the font (see A).

A Construct the font, using a plaster pillar for the column and making the bowl from white modelling paste.

B Make sure that the bowl is completely dry before you attach it otherwise it will not keep its shape.

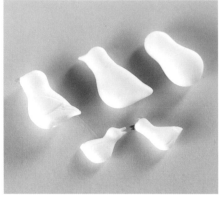

C Make some of the bluebirds with closed beaks, others with open beaks and three with tucked wings.

D The wings are shaped with a cocktail stick and must be attached to the bodies while they are still soft.

E Use a fine paintbrush to paint the birds a subtle blue, using black for the eyes and orange for the beaks.

3   Using edible glue, stick one of the smaller circles of paste onto a larger one and attach these to the bottom of the pillar (the largest forms the base). Set aside to dry for 24 hours.

4   When dry, remove the bowl from the former and attach to the top of the font with a little royal icing (see B on page 50). Leave to dry.

Bluebirds

5   Roll a size 18 ball of white paste into a cone 2.5cm (1in) long. To form a neck, roll the paste a third of the way down from the tip of the cone. Form a small peak at the bottom of the cone for a tail. For the beak, pinch a small quantity of paste at the front of the head into a point. For an open beak, cut this point carefully down the centre. Mark holes on either side of the head for the eyes. Make five more bodies using the above method, some with open and some with closed beaks (see C). Three of the birds have tucked wings; for this, cut a V shape into both sides of the bodies. Make eight smaller, flatter versions to go around the side of the cake: four facing right and four facing left. Set aside to dry for 24 hours.

6   To make a wing, form a size 6 ball into a cone 1cm (1/2in) long. Place a cocktail stick on one side of the cone and flatten it in a semi-circular motion. Repeat to form another wing but this time start the flattening action from the other side to form the second wing of the pair (see D). Attach the wings to the body with edible glue, while they are still soft, blending the joins at the centre of the back. Repeat to

make further sets of wings and attach them to two of the dried bodies. Allow the bodies to dry on foam, supporting the wings if necessary. Paint the birds blue, leaving the chest white; paint the eyes black and beak orange (see E).

Side decoration

7 Scribe clouds and branches onto the centre of each quarter section on the cake side, using the templates on page 102 (see F). Paint pale blue around the outside edge of the clouds. Pipe around the outline of the clouds with soft peak royal icing and a no.2 tube (tip). With a damp paintbrush, gently draw some of the icing down to the base of the clouds (see G).

8 Pipe along the scribed line for the branches, using dark brown royal icing and a no.1 tube. For the leaves, pipe small bulbs of green icing in groups of twos and threes.

9 Attach two of the flat bluebirds to the centre of each cloud with soft peak royal icing (see H). Pipe two tiny legs under each bird. Pipe branches and leaves on part of the base of the dried font and part way up one side.

10 Attach the font to the top of the cake with royal icing. Fill it with piping gel and allow this partly to skin over. Sit two bluebirds in the gel and attach the other three to the edge of the font with royal icing. Pipe drops of gel onto the cake to represent spilt water. Attach the white ribbon around the base and pipe a snail trail with soft peak royal icing and a no.2 tube. Attach the blue ribbon to the cake board edge.

F With the aid of a template, the sides of the cake are attractively decorated with clouds and branches.

G Use brush embroidery to give the clouds a raised, lacy cloud-like appearance. Draw down the icing with a paintbrush.

H Attach two of the smaller, flattened bluebirds to the centre of each cloud round the side of the cake.

A pretty cut-out pram sits like a greetings card on this pale blue oval cake. Delicate piped oriental stringwork and tiny butterflies complete the design, which is smart enough for the most formal christenings and suitable for a baby boy or a girl.

Dainty Pram

CAKE AND DECORATION

- ♥ 25cm (10in) oval cake
- ♥ 1.1kg (2¹/2lb) white sugarpaste (rolled fondant)
- ♥ apricot glaze or clear alcohol (gin or vodka)
- ♥ 900g (2lb) almond paste
- ♥ 115g (4oz) soft peak royal icing
- ♥ 1kg (2¹/4lb) pale blue sugarpaste
- ♥ 25g (1oz) white modelling paste
- ♥ edible glue
- ♥ white flower paste (gum paste)
- ♥ 1m (3ft) 1cm (¹/2in) wide white ribbon

SPECIAL EQUIPMENT

- ♥ 33cm (13in) oval cake board
- ♥ templates (see page 101)
- ♥ no. 1 piping tube (tip)
- ♥ piping bags
- ♥ scriber
- ♥ miniature butterfly cutter (KB)
- ♥ 3cm (1¹/4in) and 2cm (³/4in) round cutters (KB)

A Use a template to scribe the scallop design onto the sides and ends of the cake, then commence piping.

B Pipe a second row of loops to hang just below the first one. Repeat on each of the four sections.

Preparing the cake and board

1 Cover the cake board with white sugarpaste (rolled fondant), using a smoother to ensure an even finish. Set aside to dry. Brush the cake with apricot glaze or alcohol (gin or vodka). whichever you prefer, and cover with almond paste. Leave to dry. Brush the almond paste with alcohol, then cover with pale blue sugarpaste. Leave to dry for at least 24 hours. Attach the cake to the centre of the board with a little royal icing.

Oriental stringwork

2 Using the template on page 101, scribe the scalloped design onto the cake. Mark the sides of the cake with the full design, but mark only the top section on the ends. Fill a

piping bag fitted with a no. 1 tube (tip) with royal icing, and pipe large bulbs to the points of the scribed scallops on each of the four sections on the cake. Pipe a line around each section from dot to dot following the scribed markings (see A on page 54).

3 Go back to where you started, and pipe a second line from point to point around the cake. This line should hang approximately 1cm (^{1}/2in) below the first (see B on page 54) Continue until you have completed a second row all around the cake.

4 Pipe a third row of loops starting in the middle on every alternate second loop (see C).

5 Pipe five dots in between the loops in the centre of each section and three between the others. Take care not to damage the loops; they are very fragile.

Butterflies

6 From white modelling paste, cut out several tiny butterflies with the miniature cutter (see D). Set them aside to dry on folded card.

Pram

7 Using the template on page 101, cut out two pram shapes from white modelling paste, rolled out to a thickness of approximately 2mm (^{1}/14in). NOTE: When cutting out shapes from modelling paste, ensure that your craft knife has a clean, sharp blade. Wipe the blade frequently so there is no build-up of paste residue. It is also useful to spread a little white fat onto your

C Pipe a third row on every second loop. Add little dots between loops in each section, as shown.

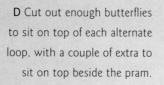

D Cut out enough butterflies to sit on top of each alternate loop, with a couple of extra to sit on top beside the pram.

E Cut out two prams from white modelling paste, using the template, then cut out the wheels with a ring cutter.

non-stick board before rolling out the paste. This will hold the paste in position while you cut out the pram shapes.

8   Using the two sizes of ring cutters, cut out wheels from the one of the prams (see E).

9   Frill the front edge of the hood of the pram on which you have cut out wheels (for frilling advice, see Fabric Effects, pages 92–3), and mark the frame as shown (see F).

10   Roll out a small piece of white flower paste (gum paste) very thinly, and cut 16 thin strips. Paint edible glue around the outline of the wheels and attach four thin strips across each of the four wheels to form spokes (see G). Set the pram sections aside to dry on foam for at least 48 hours.

11   Join one pram section to the other with a small strip of paste. While the strip is still soft, stand the pram up and allow it to dry slightly opened out, like a greetings card (see H).

Assembly

12   Position the pram on the top of the cake carefully and place one or two butterflies beside it. Attach the ribbon round the edge of the cake board with a little glue or double-sided tape.

Variation

Although I have used a pram shape for this cake, other shapes would also work. A rocking horse or crib shape would look very pretty, and the colours can be changed as appropriate.

F Frill the hood of the pram and make creases in the hood and an indentation to mark where it joins the pram.

G Make four spokes from thin strips of white flower paste and attach them to the outer edges of the wheels.

H Use a small strip of paste to attach the two sections of the pram and leave it slightly open to resemble a greetings card.

The christening robe, bonnet and bootees on this cake are so perfectly detailed that they look real. The pleating and draping require patience, but the end result is an eye-catching centrepiece for any christening.

Fit for a Princess

CAKE AND DECORATION

- ♥ 25cm (10in) long by 20cm (8in) wide rectangular cake
- ♥ apricot glaze or clear alcohol (gin or vodka)
- ♥ 950g (2¼lb) almond paste
- ♥ 900g (2lb) pale pink sugarpaste (rolled fondant)
- ♥ 350g (12oz) white sugarpaste
- ♥ 450g (1lb) white modelling paste
- ♥ edible glue
- ♥ pink food colouring

SPECIAL EQUIPMENT

- ♥ 33cm (13in) by 28cm (11in) rectangular cake board
- ♥ large embosser (J)

Preparing the cake

1 Brush the cake with apricot glaze or alcohol (gin or vodka), then cover with almond paste. Leave to dry. Brush with alcohol, then cover just the top with white sugarpaste. Roll out some pink sugarpaste (rolled fondant) and cut out two sections to cover the ends of the cake first. Make a template to ensure an accurate fit. The side and end templates should be 1cm (½in) deeper than the cake, so that when finished, the cake looks like an open box without a lid. Allow these pieces to set for about one hour before attaching to the cake sides with edible glue.

2 Make a template for the sides of the cake allowing for the thickness of the added end sections. Cut the sides from rolled pink sugarpaste using the template (see A).

A Use a template to cut the sides and ends of the box to ensure an accurate fit, and smooth them down carefully.

B Gather the skirt of the robe, making the pleats as realistic as you can. Think of the way soft fabric drapes and flows.

Set aside to dry for one hour then glue each of the pieces to the sides of the cake. Use a smoother to ensure a good finish. NOTE: If it is difficult to achieve a smooth finish, add 5ml (1 tsp) glycerine to every 450g (1lb) sugarpaste.

Christening robe

3 Roll out a large piece of white modelling paste 30cm (12in) long and 20cm (8in) wide. Emboss the hem of the robe and frill the edge with a celstick. Pleat and gather up the top of the skirt (see B on page 58). (For detailed instructions on pleating and frilling, see Fabric Effects, pages 92–3.) While still soft, attach the skirt to the top of the box and drape a little over one end.

4 Flatten a ball of paste and frill at one end to form padding for the bodice. For the bodice, roll out a piece of white paste and cut an oblong 20cm (8in) long and 10cm (4in) wide. Cut this piece in two and emboss and frill the edges as for the hem of the skirt (see C).

5 While still soft, attach the padding to the top of the skirt and wrap the bodice sides around. Brush edible glue onto the underside of the bodice to ensure it stays in position.

6 Cut and frill two 7.5cm (3in) circles for the sleeves and also a 5cm (2in) circle for the collar (see D). Gather up the sleeves and attach to either side of the bodice.

7 Cut a V shape out of the collar and fold over the top of the bodice. Attach the collar,

C Form the bodice and padding from white modelling paste and emboss the edges then frill them with a celstick.

D Cut circles to form the sleeves and collar then frill them and gather them as shown. Cut a small V out of the collar.

E Attach the padding then fix the bodice, collar and sleeves to the cake. Handle the pieces very carefully.

folding it over the neck of the bodice, and arrange the sleeves (see E). Once the frilled sleeves, bodice and skirt edges have dried, they will be extremely brittle, so handle with care.

Bootees

8 Roll two size 28 balls of paste into short cones. Flatten slightly and emboss the front. Pierce a large hole at the narrow end of the flattened cone. Cut and frill two 3.5cm (1¹/₂in) circles. Glue these to the back of the bootees and coax the centres down into the holes to form the openings (see F).

F Form the bootees from short cones of paste and emboss the fronts. Add frills around the holes for the ankles.

Bonnet

9 Roll and cut a piece of paste 15cm (6in) long and 7.5cm (3in) wide. Emboss and frill as before. Pleat and gather up very tightly before folding in half (see G). Colour a small amount of modelling paste pale pink and roll and cut two ribbons. Glue the ribbons to the bonnet and attach it to the cake.

G Cut the baby's bonnet then emboss and frill it. Cut two ribbons from some modelling paste coloured pale pink.

Finishing touches

10 Colour a small amount of paste a darker pink. Roll and cut a variety of sizes of squares. Fold these loosely and tuck them into the box so that they look like tissue paper packaging (see H).

H Attach the bonnet and add sheets of pink tissue paper, made from paste that is a few shades darker than the ribbons.

Variation

To adjust this cake design to suit a baby boy, either make the robe and cake sides white and the ribbon and tissue pieces blue, or make the robe and ribbons white and the box sides and tissue paper blue.

Nestled in a flower crib, this gorgeous baby will have everyone cooing. Refer to the Modelling Babies section (see pages 66–8) for extra tips on how to obtain good results. The roses are not too difficult to make if you have the recommended cutters.

Delicate Rose Crib

CAKE AND DECORATION

- ♥ 700g (1lb 7oz) white sugarpaste (rolled fondant)
- ♥ 20cm (8in) oval cake
- ♥ apricot glaze or clear alcohol (gin or vodka)
- ♥ 550g (1¼lb) almond paste
- ♥ 15ml (1 tbsp) pink royal icing
- ♥ 1.5m (5ft) pink picot edge ribbon
- ♥ 25g (1oz) each of pink and green flower paste (gum paste)
- ♥ 25g (1oz) brown modelling paste
- ♥ small ball of white flower paste
- ♥ edible glue

SPECIAL EQUIPMENT

- ♥ 25cm (10in) teardrop cake board
- ♥ nos. 1 and 2 piping tubes (tips)
- ♥ large all-in-one rose cutter (OP)
- ♥ styrene flower formers (CC)
- ♥ lily petal or large leaf cutter
- ♥ small calyx cutter or similar
- ♥ large leaf veiner (CC)
- ♥ Christmas rose cutter
- ♥ modelling size guide (see page 107)

A Cut two large pink roses using the large all-in-one rose cutter. Frill the edges to look like real petals.

B You can use a flower former or an apple tray to shape your roses. Attach the petals using edible glue.

Preparing the cake and board

1 Cover the cake board with white sugarpaste (rolled fondant) using a smoother to ensure an even finish. Set aside to dry.

2 Brush the cake with apricot glaze or alcohol (gin or vodka), whichever you prefer, and cover with almond paste. Leave to dry. Brush the almond paste with alcohol, then cover with white sugarpaste. Leave to dry for at least 24 hours. Attach the cake to the board with a little royal icing, positioning it in the centre. Attach ribbon around the base of the cake with edible glue. Pipe tiny dots at regular intervals over the surface of the cake with pink royal icing and a no.1 tube (tip).

Roses and crib

3 Roll out some pink flower paste (gum paste) and use a large all-in-one rose cutter to cut two large flowers. Ball and frill the edges (see A on page 62). (For frilling advice, see pages 92–3.)

4 Sit one flower into a cupped flower former or apple tray. Fix a large pink cone to a skewer and attach the petals of the remaining flower around the cone using edible glue. Glue the centre of the flower in the former, slide the other flower on the cone off the skewer and position it in the middle of the other flower (see B on page 62). Set aside your rose to dry thoroughly.

5 Cut and frill two more flowers to form the crib. Glue them together and position both in a flower former or apple tray.

Leaves and buds

6 Roll out the green flower paste and cut eight leaves using a lily petal cutter or similar large leaf cutter. Five will form a calyx and will hold the crib. Vein each leaf with a leaf veiner and allow to dry slightly curved.

7 Roll and mark two long cones for buds (see C). Leaves and buds can be coloured and glazed once they are dry.

Baby

8 For advice on making and assembling a small baby, see Modelling Babies, pages 66–8. The body is made from 15g (1/2oz) of dark brown modelling paste and the arms and legs are made from size 12 balls of paste. The head is formed

C Vein the leaves and mark the buds. It is always helpful when making flowers to have a real example close at hand.

D Mould the baby, bending the elbows and knees so that you have one right and one left version of each limb.

E Cut the baby's flower hat using pink flower paste and a Christmas rose cutter, then add a small green calyx.

from a size 20 ball (see D). Ensure that the limbs are arranged so that when the baby dries, it hardens in such a position that it will fit in the centre of the rose crib.

9 To make a hat for the baby, cut and frill two Christmas roses from pink flower paste (see E) and glue them carefully around the baby's head. Cut a small calyx using green paste and attach this to back of the hat. Attach a tiny green stem to the top of the calyx.

10 Roll and cut a small white triangle to make a nappy. Texture with either the back of a knife or a plastic pan scourer (see F). Attach the nappy to the baby with edible glue.

Assembly

11 Glue a ball of sugarpaste to one side of the top of the cake and flatten the top. Into this paste, position and glue five calyx segments. Pipe some royal icing into the centre of the calyx and carefully position the rose crib. Add thin paste ribbon strips trailing out from beneath the leaves (see G). Allow to dry. When dry, lie the baby inside the flower.

12 The other flower will sit on the cake board at the base of the cake. Use a ball of sugarpaste to hold it in position and arrange the remaining leaves and the buds into the paste. Position the finished rose into the paste (see H).

13 To finish the cake, pipe a snail trail around the base with soft peak royal icing and a no.2 tube (tip) (see H).

F You can imitate the texture of a baby's towelling nappy by pressing a plastic pan scourer onto the paste.

G Position the flower crib on top of the cake, slightly to one side, and position the baby inside the flower.

H Position the rose on the cake board, surrounded by dark green foliage, then pipe a snail trail around the base of the cake.

Modelling Babies

As babies are an obvious choice for many christening, nursery or naming celebration cakes, I have included this separate modelling section to help you achieve good results when moulding parts of the baby's body. A medium to firm modelling paste should be used: 50% sugarpaste (rolled fondant) and 50% flower paste (gum paste) kneaded together gives a medium paste, although it does depend on the firmness of the flower paste. For a firm paste, which I recommend for standing figures, use a 25% sugarpaste and 75% flower paste mixture. Rubbing a tiny amount of white vegetable fat on your fingertips sometimes helps to achieve a smooth finish.

If you can work fast, you may like to knead a small amount of gum tragacanth (or substitute) into each piece of paste immediately before you begin. This will ensure that your pieces set rock hard. The paste does start to stiffen up almost immediately, however, so you must be able to model quickly. I have not given specific sizes below because these instructions are for general use, and will need to be adapted for individual projects.

Hands

1 Roll a ball of firm modelling paste into a smooth, short cone. Flatten the cone, particularly at the rounded end (at what will be the fingertips). Leave the narrow end slightly thicker, as this will become the wrist. Now cut through the flattened cone, as shown, to make the fingers. Fingernails and knuckles can be marked using a drinking straw cut at a 45° angle (see A).

Arms

2 Form a ball of modelling paste into a sausage shape that is slightly narrower at one end. Now roll and thin the paste in between your index fingers a little way up the sausage shape from the narrow end to make a wrist. Bend the arm slightly in the middle and gently pinch one

A Make simple hands quite easily by following the steps shown above. Mark fingernails and knuckles with a straw.

B Check the cake you are making to see the position of the arms and the curve you will need at the elbow.

C When making legs, remember to add little creases at the knee and mark toenails on each toe.

D Make holes in the body for arm and leg sockets. Use softened modelling paste to attach the limbs.

E It is easier to make the back and front of the head separately from a half head mould than to make a full head.

side to form an elbow. Flatten the narrow end to make a hand, and cut as shown in the previous step. Pinch a little peg on the inside of the upper arm and this will fit into a socket on the body (see B).

Legs

3 The first stages of the leg are very similar to the arm, but more paste is used to give a bigger limb. Roll a sausage shape, making it thinner at one end, to form an ankle. Flatten the end and bend it over to make a foot. Mark or cut the toes, and bend the leg in the centre,

These cute babies are displayed on the Little Angels cake on page 28.

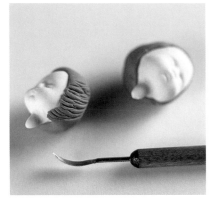

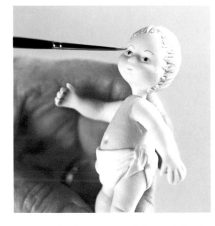

F Apply a layer of paste over the head then mark it with a curved-blade tool.

G Paint the features carefully with food colours and a fine sable paintbrush.

H Paint the hair with a diluted darker colour to give a realistic look.

pinching the paste to form a knee. Pinch little pegs at the top of the legs as instructed before (see C on page 66).

Bodies

4 Roll a large cone of paste, and pinch either side of the base to form leg sockets. Push a celstick or skewer into the top, sides and base of the cone to form sockets for the neck, legs and arms (see D on page 67).

5 The limbs can be attached to the body either soft, as long as they are handled carefully, or when they are hard. Royal icing is ideal for sticking the parts together. If you are dressing the baby, this is usually done before the limbs are attached.

Heads

6 Heads can either be made freehand or with a mould (see E on page 67). When using a mould, ensure that the paste can be removed freely. A very thin brushing of white vegetable fat can help. I usually form a small point at the front of a ball of paste and try to push this into the nose part of the mould. Press very hard without moving the paste in the mould. The surplus paste can either be moulded into the back of the head or cut off and half a head made, to which you can add more paste when the front of the head is dry. For a baby in a crib, I often just make the front of the head, as the back will not be seen on the finished cake.

7 Hair can either be painted onto a solid head or added in the form of paste. Mould a ball of paste around the back of the head and down onto the head. Mark the hair with a knife or curved-blade modelling tool (see F). This needs to be done carefully to make the hair look realistic.

8 Use edible food colours and a very fine sable brush to paint the eyes, nose and mouth (see G). You may find it easier to achieve finer details by using magnifying glasses.

9 When the hair is dry, paint the coloured paste with a darker colour (diluted) to give a shaded effect like real hair (see H).

The sweet little baby and bunny look snug on this bright cake. Either use ribbon or a strip of christening wrapping paper round the bottom of the cake. I used the colours in the paper for the baby's cover and other details.

Sleepy Pals

CAKE AND DECORATION

550g (1¹/₄lb) ivory sugarpaste
(rolled fondant)
20cm (8in) heart-shaped cake
apricot glaze or clear alcohol
(gin or vodka)
450g (1lb) almond paste
25g (1oz) lemon modelling paste
15g (¹/₂oz) flesh modelling paste
10g (¹/₃oz) pea-sized pieces of
pink and lilac modelling paste
edible glue
1m (3ft) 1cm (¹/₂in) wide ivory
ribbon
christening wrapping paper or
ribbon

SPECIAL EQUIPMENT

28cm (11in) heart-shaped
cake board
modelling size guide
(see page 107)
miniature heart-shaped cutter

Preparing the cake and board

1 Cover the cake board with ivory sugarpaste (rolled fondant), using a smoother to ensure an even surface finish. Set aside to dry. Brush the cake with apricot glaze or alcohol (gin or vodka) and cover with almond paste. Leave to dry. Brush the paste with alcohol, then cover with ivory sugarpaste. Leave to dry for 24 hours. Attach the cake to the centre of the board with royal icing.

Baby

2 To make the baby's body, mould a cone from a size 24 ball of lemon paste. With flesh modelling paste, make a little head from a size 20 ball, and also a tiny hand (see A). (For advice on making heads and hands, see Modelling Babies, pages 66–8.)

A Make the baby's body from lemon paste and its head and little hand from flesh modelling paste, then mark eyes, nose, mouth, ears and fingers.

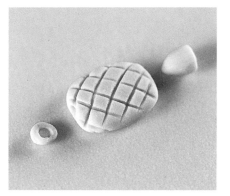

B Make the hot water bottle with pink paste. There are three parts: an oblong, a tiny ball and a cone. Score with a craft knife.

C Cut the cover and pillow from yellow paste. Make the rabbit's head and hand from lilac paste. Cut several little heart shapes.

Hot-water bottle

3 From pink paste, mould a tiny oblong for the hot-water bottle. Score the top with the back of the craft knife to give a quilted effect (see B on page 69). Make a tiny ball and push a cocktail stick through it to make a loop for the bottom of the bottle. A small cone opened out forms the top. Attach both pieces with edible glue.

Cover and pillow

4 For the cover, roll and cut out an oblong 7.5cm (3in) long and 6cm (2½in) wide from yellow paste. Mould a size 28 ball of yellow paste into a 5cm (2½in) by 3.5cm (1½in) oblong for the pillow (see C).

D Glue on the pillow then cover the baby's body and attach it. Tuck the rabbit under the cover at one side.

5 Make the tiny rabbit's head and hand from lilac paste (see Twins' Slumber, page 87, for instructions on making rabbits).

Assembly

6 While still soft, glue the pillow to one side of the top of the cake. Wrap the cover over the baby's body and attach. Tuck the rabbit into one side of the cover (see D). Let the rabbit's paw and the baby's hand curve over the top.

E Attach the paper strip or ribbon, then dot tiny hearts over the cake, placing one on the pillow.

7 Glue the thin ribbon around the edge of the cake board. Attach a strip of christening paper or a ribbon with a christening theme round the base of the cake with edible glue (see E).

8 From pink and lilac paste, cut out several tiny hearts and dot them around the sides. Place the hot-water bottle on the cover and a heart on the pillow to complete this sweet cake.

Jumbo the baby elephant is sleeping peacefully on top of this pretty cake, surrounded by a lovely frieze of toys in a woodland setting. Include models of some of your baby's favourite toys for a personal touch; colour schemes can be changed to suit.

Jumbo Junior's Nap

CAKE AND DECORATION

- 25cm (10in) teardrop cake
- 1kg (2¼lb) ivory sugarpaste (rolled fondant)
- apricot glaze or clear alcohol (gin or vodka)
- 900g (2lb) almond paste
- 15ml (1 tbsp) royal icing
- 25g (1oz) brown modelling paste
- 50g (2oz) peach modelling paste
- 75g (3oz) pale blue modelling paste
- 30g (1¼oz) white modelling paste
- edible glue
- 1m (3ft) 1cm (½in) wide peach ribbon

SPECIAL EQUIPMENT

- 33cm (13in) oval cake board
- plaque cutter (OP)
- miniature butterfly cutter (KB)
- toy cutter (FMM)
- template (see page 103)

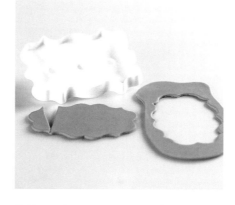

A Use a plaque cutter to cut the headboard and bottom of the bed from brown modelling paste.

B Mark stripes on the headboard and bottom of the bed and use a cutter to make a small butterfly shape in each.

Preparing the cake and board

1 Cover the cake board with ivory sugarpaste (rolled fondant), using a smoother to ensure an even finish. Set aside to dry. Brush the cake with apricot glaze or alcohol (gin or vodka) and cover with almond paste. Leave to dry. Brush with alcohol, then cover with ivory sugarpaste. When dry, attach to the oval board with a little royal icing.

Bed

2 Roll out the brown modelling paste and cut out a plaque shape with the plaque cutter (see A). Cut a small section off one end to form the headboard. Repeat, and cut another shorter section for the bottom of the bed.

C Mould the base of the bed and the pillows from peach paste then make a sheet and drape it over the end of the bed.

D Assemble the bed by sticking the headboard and bottom onto the base then arrange the pillows.

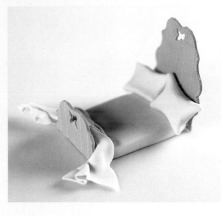

E Mould the elephant's body and legs from pale blue modelling paste. Make indentations for leg sockets.

3 Mark the sections of the bed to look like wooden planks, and cut out a butterfly shape from the top of each section (see B on page 72).

4 For the base of the bed, mould a thick rectangle 7.5cm (3in) long and 5cm (2in) wide from peach modelling paste. Make two pillows, 2.5cm (1in) by 3.5cm (1½in), in the same way. Roll and cut a peach sheet the same size as the bed base, gather it up and position it across the bottom of the bed (see C).

5 Attach the headboard and bottom section to either end of the bed with royal icing, and also position and attach the pillows (see D).

Elephant

6 The body of the elephant is made from a 25g (1oz) ball of pale blue modelling paste (size 34). Roll the ball into a fat cone about 5cm (2in) long. Pinch either side of the fat end of the cone to form sockets to hold the legs.

7 To make the legs, roll four size 17 balls of blue paste into 2.5cm (1in) sausage shapes (see E). Score wrinkles along each leg with a knife. Mark toe-nails with a drinking straw cut at a 45° angle.

8 For the head, mould a 15g (½oz) ball of paste (size 26) into a cone. Carefully roll to extend the narrow end of the cone to form a trunk. Mark wrinkles on the trunk and pierce a hole in the end. Use the drinking straw to mark semi-circles on the face so that he looks as though he is asleep.

9 For the ears, flatten two size 14 balls of blue paste until they measure approximately 2.5cm (1in) across (see F). Brush a small amount of glue onto either side of the head and press the ears gently into the head, curling the top of each ear gently forward.

10 When the head is dry, outline the eye socket and paint eyelashes. Outline the toenails carefully. Assemble the elephant while the pieces are still soft and attach him to the bed with royal icing.

Side decoration

11 Roll out some white modelling paste quite thinly, and cut out several toys using toy cutters (see G). Allow to dry. With the same paste, mould a tiny baby's bottle and place it between the elephant's feet, as though Junior is holding it.

12 Using the templates on page 103, roll out and cut sky sections from blue modelling paste, trees from brown modelling paste and clumps of grass from peach modelling paste. Make sure you cut enough to go right around the base of the cake. With edible glue, fix these at intervals around the side of the cake to form the background then position the toys as you want them (see H).

Assembly

13 Attach the bed to one end of the cake with royal icing. Stick the peach ribbon around the edge of the cake board with glue or double-sided tape.

F Make the elephant's head from pale blue modelling paste and mark features on it. Make the ears and let them dry curved.

G Cut out a selection of toys from white modelling paste. Make a baby's bottle from a sausage shape of white paste.

H Cut the sky background, the trees and grass, then fix them round the side of the cake, arranging the toys on top.

The beautiful draped lace of this crib shows the versatility of modelling paste to great effect. Spend time working with the paste to ensure the lace drapes look like real fabric. Its fine detailing is complemented by the piped lace.

Draped Lace Crib

CAKE AND DECORATION

- ♥ 1kg (2¼lb) white sugarpaste (rolled fondant)
- ♥ 25cm (10in) petal cake
- ♥ apricot glaze or clear alcohol (gin or vodka)
- ♥ 900g (2lb) almond paste
- ♥ 115g (4oz) royal icing
- ♥ 15g (½oz) white modelling paste
- ♥ 15g (½oz) flesh modelling paste
- ♥ small piece of pink modelling paste
- ♥ edible glue
- ♥ 1.25m (4ft) of white, pink or blue ribbon for the board

SPECIAL EQUIPMENT

- ♥ 33cm (13in) round cake board
- ♥ piping bag with no. 1 tube (tip)
- ♥ lace template (see page 103)
- ♥ plastic lace
- ♥ oval cutter or template (see page 102)
- ♥ modelling size guide (see page 107)
- ♥ baby head mould (HP)

Preparing the cake and board

1 Cover the cake board with white sugarpaste (rolled fondant) using a smoother to ensure an even surface finish. Set aside to dry. Brush the cake with apricot glaze or alcohol (gin or vodka), whichever you prefer, and cover with almond paste. Leave to dry. Brush the almond paste with alcohol, then cover with white sugarpaste. Leave to dry for at least 24 hours. Attach the cake to the centre of the cake board with a little royal icing.

Lace design

2 With soft peak royal icing and a no. 1 tube (tip), pipe a lace design at the top edge of the cake around each scallop (see A). A wide variety of lace designs can be

A Using soft peak royal icing, pipe your chosen lace design round the top edge of the cake, following the scallop shapes.

B Cut squares of white modelling paste for the tail pieces and emboss them with a lace design using plastic lace.

interpreted for piping onto cakes. (For lace design, see Templates, page 103.) Finish off the design with pink dots.

Tails

3 Texture the white modelling paste by placing a piece of plastic lace over the square and press and roll firmly over it with a rolling pin (see B on page 76). Use even pressure. Cut out a 7.5cm (3in) square of lace-embossed paste.

C Frill the squares, and then pleat so that they look as if they are hanging softly in folds (see page 92 for pleating advice).

4 Fold in the edges on two sides of the square and frill the other two. Using a skewer, form pleats from corner to corner (see C). (For detailed instructions on pleating, see Fabric Effects, pages 92–3). Make five further tails.

D Attach the tails to the cake while they are still soft, otherwise you will have difficulty getting them to adhere.

5 While they are still soft, attach the tails with edible glue to the top edge of the cake in the recess between each piped section (see D).

Baby

6 Use a size 26 ball of pale flesh modelling paste to make a baby's head. Do this freehand or use a mould (see Modelling Babies, pages 66–8), then paint on the features. For the bonnet, roll and cut a 3.5cm (1½in) circle of white modelling paste. Frill the edges and attach it to the baby's head with edible glue, folding the frilled edge around the face (see E).

E Use a mould to make the baby's head from flesh modelling paste, then add a frilled white bonnet.

Crib

7 Detailed instructions on how to make this crib can be found on pages 40–2. Please note that the quantities given there can be varied, depending on the size of the cake and whether the crib is to be a small decoration or a large feature. If the crib is to have tall drapes made of paste, then obviously you will need to increase the amount of paste. I have used an oval shape for this crib (using the template on page 102) but you could choose any shape you like. Use a piece of plastic lace to emboss the paste to give a lace effect. It is advisable to dry the canopy and crib sections on foam. As air is trapped in the foam, this allows the top and bottom of the paste to dry simultaneously.

Blanket and pillow

8 Using an oval cutter or the template on page 102, roll and cut two ovals from white modelling paste. Frill the edges. Cut one in half for the pillow, and cut the second a third of the way down. Fold over the top edge of the largest piece to form a blanket (see F).

9 Position the pillow and blanket pieces on top of the crib before adding the canopy (see G). Support with foam from underneath while drying. Attach the baby's head to the pillow with royal icing.

Finishing touches

10 Trim the top of the crib with a frilled white strip and arrange a little bow made from pink or blue modelling paste on top of the canopy at the front (see H).

11 The cake board can be trimmed with white, pink or blue ribbon. Attach it with glue or double-sided tape.

F Frill the edges of both the oval blanket and the pillow, and attach the baby's head securely with royal icing.

G Assemble the crib, attaching all the pieces with royal icing, then place the canopy carefully over the top.

H For a finishing touch, make a little bow from pink modelling paste and position it on top of the canopy at the front.

A very apt design for a new arrival, anticipated so eagerly for so long. Your personal greeting or name could be easily added to the clouds of steam. The train is easier to make than it looks, since there are templates for each of the pieces.

New Arrival

CAKE AND DECORATION

- 1kg (2¹/4lb) ivory sugarpaste (rolled fondant)
- 25cm (10in) hexagonal cake
- apricot glaze or clear alcohol (gin or vodka)
- 900g (2lb) almond paste
- 25g (1oz) each of green, lilac and lemon modelling paste
- 15g (¹/2oz) flesh modelling paste
- brown food colouring
- 115g (4oz) royal icing
- 25g (1oz) white modelling paste
- edible glue
- 1.5m (5ft) 1cm (¹/2in) wide lilac ribbon.

SPECIAL EQUIPMENT

- 33cm (13in) hexagonal cake board
- cutting wheel (PME)
- templates (see page 104)
- 1.8cm (³/4in), 2.5cm (1in) and 2.8cm (1¹/4in) ring cutters (KB)

A Roughen the texture of the paste on the cake board to create the ground that the railway track will run across.

B Cut out small green wheels and lilac railway carriages for the back section of each of the trains.

Preparing the cake and board

1 Cover the cake board with ivory sugarpaste (rolled fondant). Use a sharp knife to texture the sugarpaste (see A). Set aside to dry. Brush the cake with apricot glaze or alcohol (gin or vodka), whichever you prefer, and cover with almond paste. Leave to dry. Brush the almond paste with alcohol, then cover with ivory sugarpaste. Leave to dry for at least 24 hours. Attach the cake to the board, positioning it in the centre.

Train

2 Roll out a piece of green modelling paste and cut out two small wheels for each carriage. You will require 16 small green wheels. With the lilac paste, roll out and

cut eight carriages, four small wheels and two large wheels, using different sizes of ring cutters (see B on page 80).

3 Using the templates on page 104, cut out two sets of train engines and carriages using the green paste and a sharp, thin-blade craft knife. Rub a little white fat onto the board to hold the paste in position while you are cutting. A cutting wheel is also useful when you are cutting out curves. Roll out a small amount of lemon paste and cut two roof sections (see C). Set aside all these pieces to dry overnight.

C Use templates and ring cutters to make green engines with yellow roofs and lilac wheels.

Babies' faces and hands

4 Using the 1.8cm (³/₄in) ring cutter, cut 24 babies' faces from flesh modelling paste. Add a tiny nose to each face and then mark eyes and mouth with a drinking straw. To highlight the features, use diluted brown food colouring and paint over the eyes and mouth with a very fine paintbrush. Roll and flatten 48 tiny pieces of flesh modelling paste for hands (see D). NOTE: If you are making this cake for an older child, you could substitute the babies' faces for some favourite toys your child will recognize.

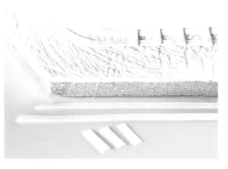

D Cut the babies' faces from flesh modelling paste and paint on their excited expressions.

Railway track

5 For the railway track, roll out and cut long strips of lemon modelling paste 3mm (¹/₈in) wide. Attach the first strip on the board up against the base of the cake side. Repeat to complete the first strip around the cake. Roll and cut further strips and attach these to the

E The yellow railway track runs right around the base of the cake. Place sleepers across it at regular intervals.

board also, leaving a 1cm (1/2in) gap between the two strips.

6 Roll and cut further strips of paste the same width as before, but this time cut these into 2.5cm (1in) lengths and lay them at intervals across the two lengths of track around the board to form sleepers (see E).

Attaching the train

7 Using soft peak royal icing, attach the engine sections and wheels to two opposite sides of the hexagonal cake, and stick two carriages with wheels to each of the four remaining sides (see F).

8 Attach one or two babies' faces and hands to the top of each carriage with soft peak royal icing (see G). Vary the positions a little.

Smoke trail

9 Roll out some white modelling paste, slightly thicker than for the train. Using the cutting wheel and the templates on page 104, cut out three smoke trail sections (see H).

10 With edible glue, attach the largest section of smoke to the top of the cake so that it looks as though it is coming from the funnel of one of the trains. Attach the further two sections above this one.

11 A greeting or name can be added to the smoke at this stage if required. Attach the lilac ribbon to the edge of the cake board with glue or double-sided tape.

F Attach the engine to the cake, with the wheels overlapping, roof on top and the funnel at the front.

G Attach the babies' faces and hands on top of the carriages, looking as though they are peering out at the view.

H Cut smoke trails using the template and attach them so that they appear to be drifting up from the funnels.

This attractive cake is magically turned into a beautiful crib for two sleeping babies and their cuddly rabbits. This would be a perfect christening cake to make for twin babies and the colours can be changed for boys or girls.

Twins' Slumber

CAKE AND DECORATION

- ♥ 550g (1¼lb) ivory sugarpaste (rolled fondant)
- ♥ 75g (3oz) pale green sugarpaste
- ♥ 18cm (7in) oval cake
- ♥ apricot glaze or clear alcohol (gin or vodka)
- ♥ 450g (1lb) almond paste
- ♥ 115g (4oz) royal icing
- ♥ 1m (3ft) ribbon
- ♥ 225g (8oz) ivory modelling paste
- ♥ edible glue
- ♥ 25g (1oz) flesh modelling paste
- ♥ 7g (¼oz) each of pink and blue modelling paste
- ♥ lustre colours (pastel shades)
- ♥ brown food colouring

SPECIAL EQUIPMENT

- ♥ 23cm (9in) and 25.5cm (10in) heart-shaped cake boards
- ♥ modelling size guide (see page 107)
- ♥ miniature embosser (FMM)

Preparing the cake and boards

1 Cover the smaller board in ivory sugarpaste (rolled fondant) and the larger one in pale green, using a smoother to ensure an even surface finish. Set aside to dry. Brush the cake with apricot glaze or alcohol (gin or vodka), and cover with almond paste. The sides and top should be covered separately to give an edge to the cake. Leave to dry for 24 hours. Attach the cake in the centre of the smaller board with a little royal icing. Place this on top of the larger board and attach the ribbon with edible glue.

Pleating

2 Make a template from thin card, which is the depth of the cake and approximately 15cm (6in) long. Roll out and cut a section of ivory modelling paste, emboss one

A Roll out some ivory modelling paste and pleat it, using a thin skewer, to give a draped effect round the sides.

B Make the blanket and pillow from ivory paste. Press indents into the pillow and mark the blanket for a quilted effect.

C Form two cones of white sugarpaste for the bodies and four balls for the feet. These will not be seen on the finished cake.

D Mould the babies' heads and hands from flesh modelling paste, marking their eyes, noses, mouths, ears and fingers.

E Lay the babies' heads side by side on the pillow, then arrange their bodies and feet in appropriate positions.

side and use a thin skewer to pleat the paste. (For detailed instructions on how to pleat, see Fabric Effects, pages 92–3.) Gently flatten one side of each pleat on the edge to ensure they stay intact when attached to the cake. Brush the cake side with edible glue and attach the pleated section (see A on page 84). Complete and attach further sections.

Pillow and blanket

3 To make the pillow, roll and cut a piece of ivory modelling paste that is 10cm (4in) square. Lay a small section of flattened paste onto one end and fold the strip over this. Glue the sides to complete the pillow (see B on page 84).

4 Glue the pillow to the top of the cake, and with your thumb press two indents for heads.

5 Make the blanket by cutting a 15cm (6in) square of ivory paste. To achieve the quilted effect, mark the paste diagonally with either a thin skewer or the edge of an icing ruler.

Twins

6 Using two size 34 balls of sugarpaste, roll two cones to form bodies. Make four size 19 balls of paste for the feet (see C).

7 Form the head using a size 14 ball of flesh modelling paste (for detailed instructions, see Modelling Babies, pages 66–8).

8 Make the hands (you need three) by forming size 7 balls of paste into flattened cones and then cutting fingers (see D).

Assembly

9 With edible glue, attach the babies' heads
to the pillow, then attach their bodies and feet
to the top of the cake. The bodies and feet will
lie underneath the blanket, marking the shapes
of the sleeping twins (see E).

10 While it is still soft, lay the blanket on top
of the babies' bodies and feet and gently mould
it around the bodies and under the heads.
Attach the hands so that they rest over the
edge of the blanket. The quilted sections of the
blanket can be painted with pastel shades of
lustre colour diluted with alcohol (see F).

F Lay the blanket over the babies
then paint its diamond pattern
with pale pastel lustre colours
diluted with alcohol.

Rabbits

11 Tiny pink and blue rabbits complete this
delightful cake. To make the pink rabbit, roll a
size 16 ball of pink modelling paste into a cone
for the body. For the arms and legs, form size
12 balls into cones. Indent two hand shapes on
the arms and mark the feet with a craft knife.
For the head, roll a size 13 ball into a long
cone. Cut and indent the narrow end to form
long ears. Use the end of a drinking straw to
mark the eyes and nose. Insert a piece of
uncooked spaghetti to attach the head firmly
to the body (see G).

G Make one pink and one blue
rabbit – or more if you wish.
Insert a piece of uncooked
spaghetti to attach the head.

H When you have assembled
your rabbits, arrange one on top
of the blanket and one on the
cake board below.

12 Paint the features carefully with brown food
colouring. Repeat with blue modelling paste to
make the other rabbit (see H).

13 Assemble the rabbits and stick them to
the cake with royal icing, positioning them so it
looks as though the twins have dropped them.

A gathered chiffon canopy gives a light and airy finish to this pretty three-tier stacked cake, suitable for any type of christening. A baby lies sleeping peacefully in a sweet crib on top of the cake surrounded by scattered peach rosebuds and maidenhair fern leaves.

Chiffon Elegance

CAKE AND DECORATION

- 50g (2oz) peach sugarpaste (rolled fondant)
- 20cm (8in), 15cm (6in) and 10cm (4in) shallow round cakes
- apricot glaze or clear alcohol (gin or vodka)
- 1kg (2¼lb) almond paste
- 1.25kg (2½lb) ivory sugarpaste
- 15g (½oz) peach flower paste (gum paste)
- 25g (1oz) white modelling paste
- 3g (⅛oz) flesh modelling paste
- edible glue
- 30ml (2 tbsp) royal icing
- ivory chiffon, 25cm (10in) square
- 1m (3ft) 1cm (½in) wide white ribbon

A Make lots of little maidenhair fern leaves from peach flower paste. These will cascade down the cake tiers.

B Make six miniature roses and buds from peach paste (these also appear on Elegant Storks on pages 24–7).

SPECIAL EQUIPMENT

- silk-effect rolling pin (OP)
- 25cm (10in) round cake board
- 15cm (6in) and 10cm (4in) cake cards
- miniature maidenhair fern cutters (KB)
- small all-in-one rose cutter (OP)
- 8cm (3in) long styrene egg
- miniature embosser
- Christmas rose cutter
- one length of white 24-gauge wire

Preparing the cakes and board

1 Roll out the peach sugarpaste (rolled fondant), texture with the silk-effect rolling pin and use to cover the cake board. Set aside to dry.

2 Brush the cakes with apricot glaze or alcohol. Attach the two smaller cakes to the cake cards and cover all cakes with almond

C Attach the roses and fern leaves, some of them clinging to a curvy white tendril that slips over the side of the cake.

D Mould the crib around a styrene egg for an authentic shape. Make curved sausage shapes for the legs.

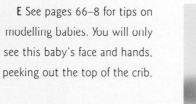

E See pages 66–8 for tips on modelling babies. You will only see this baby's face and hands, peeking out the top of the crib.

paste. Leave to dry. Brush the almond paste with alcohol, then cover all the cakes with ivory sugarpaste. Leave to dry for at least 24 hours. NOTE: Sit the small cakes and cards onto a larger board to minimize handling.

3 Attach the large cake to the board with a little royal icing and stack the other two on top using royal icing to attach them to each other.

Leaves and flowers

4 Roll out some peach flower paste (gum paste) and cut approximately 15 each of four different sizes of maidenhair fern leaves (see A on page 88). Set them aside to dry.
NOTE: Maidenhair cutters are usually sold in sets of three or four different sizes.

5 Using a small all-in-one rose or blossom cutter, make six miniature roses from peach flower paste (see B on page 88.) There are instructions for making miniature roses in Elegant Storks on page 22.

6 Attach the roses and fern leaves to the cakes, as if they are cascading down from the top tier. With soft peak royal icing and a no. 1 tube (tip), pipe trailing stems down the cake sides between the leaves (see C).

Crib

7 Mould a piece of white modelling paste around half of a styrene egg to form the oval shape of the crib. Roll two small, curved sausage shapes for the legs (see D) and attach with royal icing.

Baby

8 Use a size 14 ball of flesh modelling paste to mould a tiny head and hands. (See Modelling Babies on pages 66–8 for instructions.) Use white paste to mould a cone for the body and two tiny balls for the feet (see E).

Pillow

9 Form a small flat oblong of white modelling paste into a pillow shape and flatten and frill the edges. Roll and frill a small rectangle for the cover. Make sure that the pillow and cover will fit snugly into the crib. The cover can be embossed with a miniature embosser to give an attractive texture (see F).

Assembly

10 Using a Christmas rose cutter, cut and attach two petal shapes to create a decorative setting for the legs of the crib (see G).

11 Cut the chiffon to approximately 25cm (10in) long and 15cm (6in) wide. Sew a running stitch along one long edge and gather up. Bend the length of wire in half; this will support the canopy on the cake (see H).

12 Place the baby in the crib and stand it on the top tier of the cake. Position the wire over the crib and drape the canopy on top of it. The wire should rest on the cake but should not pierce the icing. Pipe royal icing under the bottom edge of the canopy to hold it in position. A rose can be attached to the top of the canopy with royal icing. Attach the ribbon around the cake with edible glue.

F Cut the pillow and frill its edges, then cut the blanket and emboss it with a pattern of your choice.

G Use a flower cutter to make an attractive base for the crib to rest on then stick all the pieces in place with royal icing.

H Sew the floaty ivory chiffon along one edge and gather the fabric. Bend the length of wire to support the canopy.

Fabric Effects

Frilling and pleating are ideal ways to create the impression of fabric. With care, and with practice of the following techniques, you will achieve a good result on your finished cakes.

Modelling paste is used for all the frilling and pleating throughout the book. I use a mixture of sugarpaste (rolled fondant) and flower paste (gum paste) kneaded together. I vary the ratio of one to the other depending on how strong I require the finished piece to be. I generally recommend a 50:50 ratio for draping, pleating and frilling. A 75% sugarpaste and 25% flower paste mix is fine for pleating and draping that will be attached to the cake surface, but increase the flower paste content for cut-outs, cards and free-standing pieces. Remember, the higher the proportion of flower paste, the firmer the paste and the quicker it will set.

Embossing

Embossing the surface of the paste recreates the look of lace edging and embroidery. It is a good idea to dust the paste lightly with icing sugar to ensure that the embosser is easily removed from the paste. You can rub a tiny amount of white vegetable fat (shortening) onto the embosser (this will also help with removal). Roll out the paste to the required size and thickness, and press the embosser onto the surface as evenly as you can.

NOTE: It is essential to practise embossing before making a celebration cake, for if the result is unsatisfactory you will have to start over again and remake your piece.

Frilling

Roll out the modelling paste about 1mm (1/25in) thick to the required size. With the tip of a celstick or skewer, or

Embossing: rub a little white vegetable paste onto the embosser then press it lightly but firmly onto the paste.

Frilling: use a celstick or skewer to make frills. It doesn't matter if they are slightly uneven and not equal in size.

Pleating a: pleating requires practice. Roll the paste until it is very thin and use a thin skewer to lift it.

the end of a paintbrush, roll backwards and forwards along the edge of the paste with an even pressure. The paste should lift up and form a frill. If the paste sticks to the board, lightly dust with either icing sugar or 50:50 icing (confectioner's) sugar and cornflour (cornstarch).

Pleating

1 Roll the modelling paste about 1mm ($^1/_{25}$in) thick to the required size. Slide a thin barbecue skewer underneath, and lift it until the paste either side of the skewer touches underneath. This is your first pleat. Gently pinch the paste together with your finger and thumb along the length of the skewer to ensure that the pleat stays intact.

2 Remove the skewer from the paste and press it down firmly on top of the pleat. You will now have two pleats.

3 Continue to pleat in this way until you have finished pleating the completed section. The length of the piece will vary depending on how well the section is gathered.

4 To ensure that the pleats will not come undone when lifted, press a celstick onto the top edge of the pleated piece and flatten it firmly. Trim this flat edge straight for a neater effect, especially if the top edge of the section is going to be visible. NOTE: Make sure the modelling paste is not too thick or the fabric effect will be lost.

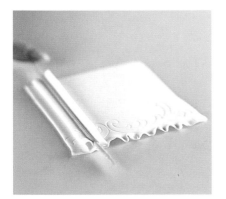

Pleating b: press the skewer or celstick firmly onto the top of the first pleat to form two separate pleats.

Pleating c: when you have finished pleating the required length of paste, it will have a concertina appearance.

Pleating d: gently press a seam along one edge to ensure your pleats don't fall out when you try to lift the paste.

This clever idea uses three separate cakes piled together with a cute bunny rabbit balanced on top. The colours of the icing on each block can be varied, perhaps using pink, lilac or green, and any toy can be chosen to sit on top.

Building Blocks

CAKE AND DECORATION

550g (1¼lb) white sugarpaste
(rolled fondant)
3 x 7.5cm (3in) square cakes
apricot glaze or clear alcohol
(gin or vodka)
900g (2lb) almond paste
edible glue
350g (12oz) each of pale blue
and pale lemon sugarpaste
25g (1oz) each of white, pale
blue and pale lemon modelling
paste
115g (4oz) soft peak royal icing

SPECIAL EQUIPMENT

25cm (10in) hexagonal
cake board
templates (pages 105–6)
rabbit ornament (TP)

Preparing the cake and board

1 Cover the cake board with white sugarpaste (rolled fondant), using a smoother to ensure an even surface finish. Set aside to dry.

2 Brush the cakes with apricot glaze or alcohol (gin or vodka), whichever you prefer, and cut squares of almond paste to cover the sides of each cake. Attach the squares and leave them to dry.

3 Measure the cake sides carefully then, using white sugarpaste, cut two squares for each cake that fit the sides exactly. Attach these squares to opposite sides of the cake with edible glue and leave them to dry.

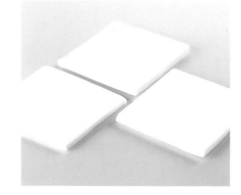

A Measure the area to be covered carefully before cutting the squares of sugarpaste to cover the sides of the cubes.

B Stick the sugarpaste squares onto the cakes with edible glue, making sure the edges sit together neatly.

C Using the template, cut fifteen letters, five in each of the three different colours you have selected.

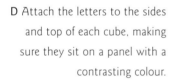

D Attach the letters to the sides and top of each cube, making sure they sit on a panel with a contrasting colour.

E You could use a teddy, a rag doll, or any animal character to decorate your cake top, or make a model from paste.

4 Using pale blue sugarpaste, cut a further two squares for each cake and attach them to opposite sides, but this time use the cake to cut a template, as you will have to allow a certain amount of extra length for the sides that have already been covered (see A on page 94).

5 To finish making the cubes, cover the remaining two sides of each cake with pale lemon squares (again using a template) (see B on page 94). Set them aside to dry.

Letters

6 Using the templates on pages 105–6, trace some letters onto card and cut them out.

7 Thinly roll out some coloured modelling paste then cut out five letters for each of the three cakes (see C). Leave to dry.

8 Using edible glue, attach the letters to the sides and top of the cubes (see D).

Assembly

9 Attach two cubes to the cake board with soft peak royal icing and position the remaining cube so that it sits on the other two.

10 The rabbit that I have used (see E) is an ornament. Position it carefully on the top building block. If you prefer, you can model a rabbit by following the instructions in Twins' Slumber, page 87. Alternatively, you could model a baby (see pages 66–8) or an elephant (see Jumbo Junior's Nap, page 74).

Basic modelling skills are all that are required for these cute bootees. If you enjoy sugar flower-making, a spray of your favourite blooms can be added; otherwise, shop-bought silk flowers can look just as effective.

Pink Bootees

CAKE AND DECORATION

- ♥ 1kg (2¹/4lb) white sugarpaste (rolled fondant)
- ♥ 25cm (10in) oval cake
- ♥ apricot glaze or clear alcohol (gin or vodka)
- ♥ 900g (2lb) almond paste
- ♥ a small amount of royal icing
- ♥ 1m (3ft) 5cm (2in) wide pink tulle ribbon
- ♥ piping gel
- ♥ 25g (1oz) white flower paste (gum paste)
- ♥ pink food colouring
- ♥ 150g (5oz) pink modelling paste
- ♥ edible glue
- ♥ silk or sugar flowers

SPECIAL EQUIPMENT

- ♥ 33cm (13in) oval cake board
- ♥ lace leaf cutter (OP)
- ♥ modelling size guide (see page 107)

Preparing the cake and board

1 Cover the cake board with white sugarpaste (rolled fondant) using a smoother to ensure an even finish. Set aside to dry. Brush the cake with apricot glaze or alcohol (gin or vodka), whichever you prefer, and cover with almond paste. Leave to dry. Brush the almond paste with alcohol, then cover with white sugarpaste. Leave to dry for at least 24 hours. Attach the cake to the board with a little royal icing, positioning it in the centre of the board.

Ribbon and lace

2 Attach the wide pink tulle ribbon around the base of the cake using a little piping gel to hold it firmly in position. The lace pieces will sit on top of this.

A Using a lace leaf cutter, cut eight lace pieces from thinly rolled white flower paste, taking care not to tear the fragile shapes.

B Using a soft paintbrush, apply pink-coloured piping gel to the areas of cake that show through the lace.

3 Roll out some white flower paste (gum paste) quite thinly and cut out eight lace pieces with a lace leaf cutter (see A on page 97).

4 Attach these to the sides of the cake and over the ribbon while they are still soft.

5 Where the cake surface shows through the lace, paint with piping gel, to which a very small quantity of pink colouring has been added (see B on page 97).

Bootees

6 Roll a size 34 ball of pink modelling paste into a cone 7.5cm (3in) long. Flatten slightly and make a hole on the top of the narrow part to form the opening of the bootee. With a narrow skewer or the back of a palette knife mark diagonal lines for a quilted effect (see C).

7 Roll out a piece of pink paste and cut a rectangle 8.5cm (3¹/₂in) by 5cm (2in). Gather the paste along one length to form the top of the bootee. Turn back the top corners (see D).

8 Using edible glue, attach the gathered top in the hole on the base of the bootee, pressing firmly inside to ensure the top sits flush. Repeat to make a second bootee (see E).

9 Roll, cut and fold two bows from white flower paste, and attach them to the bootees with edible glue. Attach the bootees to the cake with royal icing. A hand-made spray of flowers may be positioned behind the bootees for extra detail. Alternatively, silk flowers can be used.

C Create the impression of quilting by scoring the bootees with criss-crossing diagonal lines, using a palette knife.

D Score a rectangle of paste for the top of the bootees, then gather it along one length, turning back the corners.

E Attach the tops to the bases of the bootees. Make two bows from white modelling paste and attach them.

Templates

Teddy

Page 36 Up, Up and Away

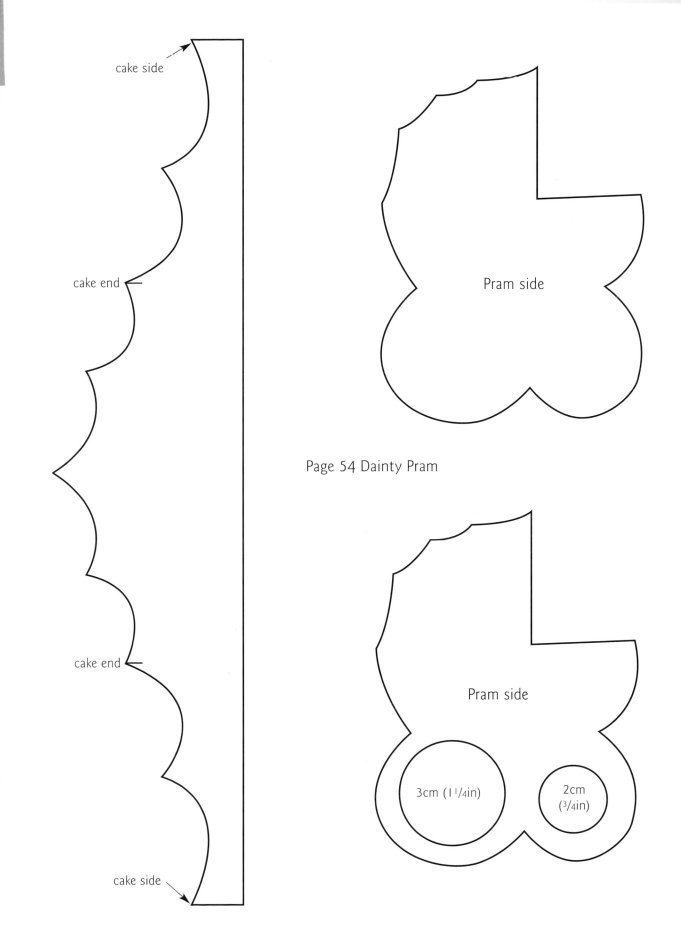

cake side

cake end

cake end

cake side

cake side

Pram side

Page 54 Dainty Pram

Pram side

3cm (1¹/4in)

2cm (³/4in)

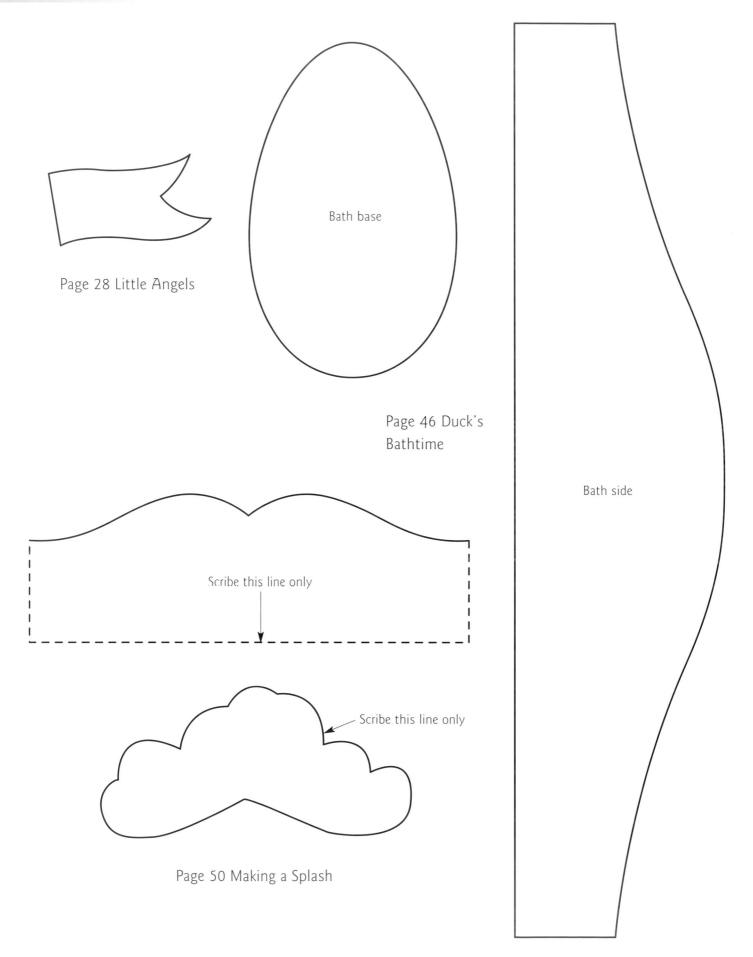

Page 28 Little Angels

Bath base

Page 46 Duck's
Bathtime

Scribe this line only

Scribe this line only

Bath side

Page 50 Making a Splash

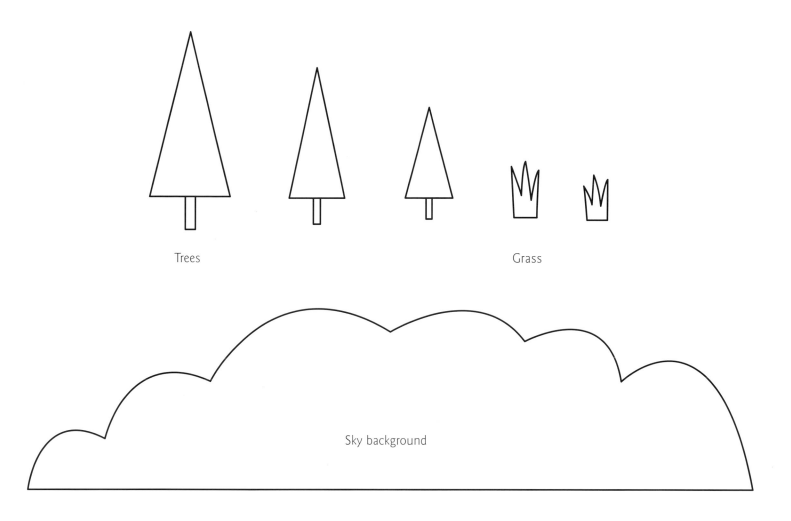

Trees

Grass

Sky background

Page 72 Jumbo Junior's Nap

Lace pattern

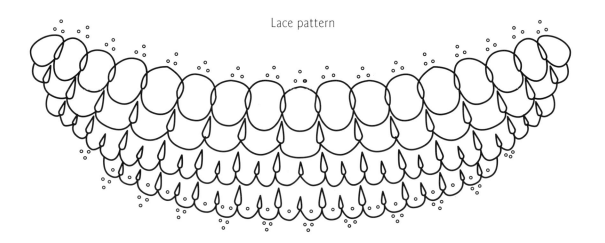

Page 76 Draped Lace Crib

Engine

Carriage

Smoke trails

Page 80 New Arrival

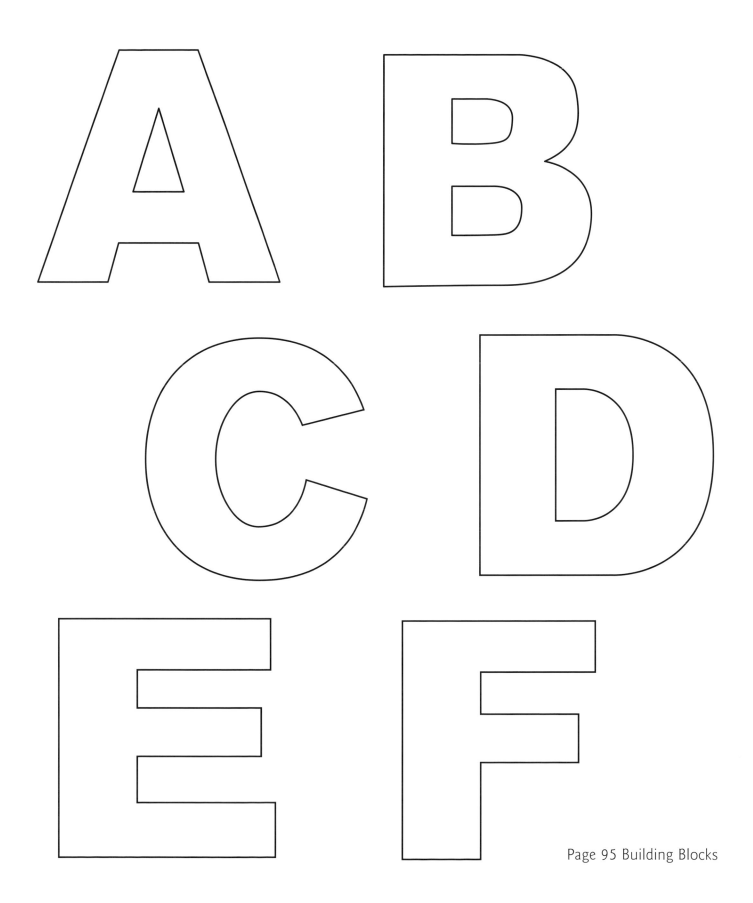

Page 95 Building Blocks

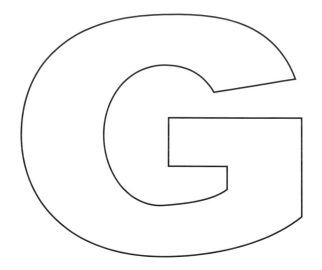

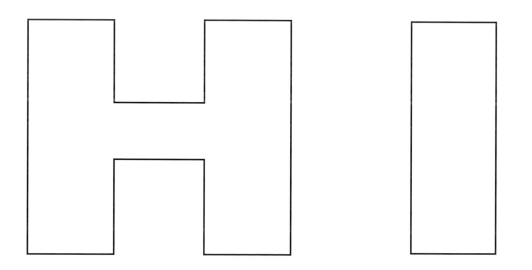

Page 95 Building Blocks

Modelling Size Guide

Trace on card and cut out circles

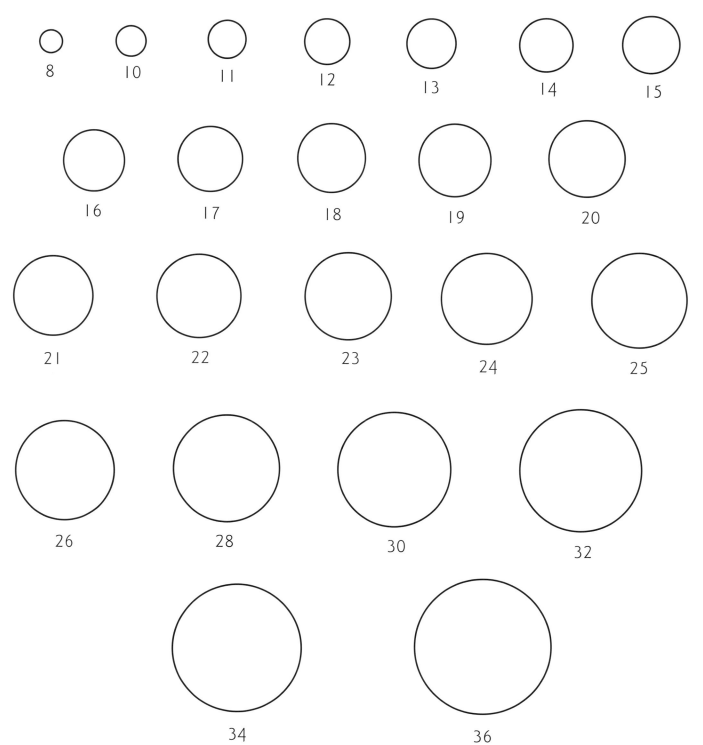

Suppliers

The author and publishers would like to thank the following for their help in the production of this book, particularly Heather Smith, George Hosgood and Terry Wood at DIY Icing Centre.

UK

DIY Icing Centre
8 Edwards Road
Erdington, Birmingham B24 9EP
Tel. 0121 384 8236
Fax. 0121 313 3127

Culpitt Cake Art
Culpitt Ltd
Jubilee Industrial Estate
Ashington
Northumberland NE63 8UQ
Tel. 01670 814545

Celcakes and Celcrafts
Springfield House
Gate Helmsley
York, North Yorks YO4 1NF
Tel. 01759 371447

Guy Paul & Co. Ltd
Unit B4, Foundry Way
Little End Road
Eaton Socon
Cambs. PE19 3JH

FMM
Unit 5 Kings Park Ind. Est.
Primrose Hill
Kings Langley
Herts. WD4 8ST
Tel. 01923 268699
Fax. 01923 261266

E.T.Webb (Cake Dummies)
18 Meadow Close
Woodley, Stockport SK6 1QZ

Holly Products (HP)
Holly Cottage
Hassall Green
Sandbach
Cheshire CW11 0YA
Tel. 01270 761403

Orchard Products (OP)
51 Hallyburton Road
Hove
East Sussex BN3 7GP
Tel. 01273 419418
Fax. 01273 412512

Renshaw Scott Ltd.
Crown Street
Liverpool L8 7RF
Tel. 0151 706 8200
(Supplier of Regalice sugarpaste used in book)

Squires Kitchen
Squires House
3 Waverley Lane
Farnham
Surrey GU9 8BB
Tel. 01252 711749

Kit Box (KB)
DRF Technical Services
1 Fernlea Gardens
Easton in Gordano
Avon BS20 0JF
Tel. & Fax. 01275 374557

Sugar City
78 Battle Road
St.Leonard's-on-Sea
E.Sussex TN37 7AG
Tel. 01424 432448
Fax. 01424 421359

Patchwork Cutters (PC)
3 Raines Close
Greasby
Wirral
Merseyside CH49 2QB
Tel./Fax. 0151 678 5053

Treasured Pals ornament:
for suppliers, see
http//www.treasuredpals.co.uk

PME Sugarcraft (PME)
Brember Road
South Harrow
Middlesex HA2 8UN
Tel. 020 8864 0888

AUSTRALIA

Cupid's Cake Decorations
2/90 Belford Street
Broadmeadow
NSW 2292
Tel. +61 2 4962 1884

Cake Decorating School
of Australia
Shop 7, Port Philip Arcade
232 Flinders Street
Melbourne
Victoria 3000
Tel. + 61 3 9654 5335

USA

Beryl's Cake Decorating
& Pastry Supplies
PO Box 1584
N. Springfield
VA22151–0584
Tel. +1 800 488 2749

Nicholas Lodge
International Sugar Art Collection
6060 McDonough Drive, Suite D

Norcross, GA 30093
Tel. +1 770 453 9449

CANADA

Creative Cutters
561 Edward Avenue, Unit 1
Richmond Hill
Ontario L4C 9W6
Tel. +1 905 883 5638

SOUTH AFRICA

JEM Cutters (J)
PO Box 115 Kloof 3640
Kwazulu Natal
Tel. +27 31 7011431

Index

almond paste 14
Alphabet Heart 33–5
angels 30–2

babies 64–5, 66–8, 69, 78, 82, 86, 91
balloons 38
banners 32, 102
bath 46, 48, 102
beads 16
bears see teddies
bed 72, 74
bib 44
Bib and Blossoms 43–5
birds 29, 30, 52–3
blossoms 43–4
bonnet 61
bootees 61, 98
brush embroidery 12, 53
bubbles 48–9
Building Blocks 94–6
buttercream 13
butterfly cutters 31, 56, 74

cake boards 15
cake recipes 12–13
Chiffon Elegance 88–91
christening robe 60
clouds 29–30, 32, 53
covering 14–15

cribs 40–2, 64–5, 78–9, 90
cutters 9
cutting 56–7

Dainty Pram 54–7
Delicate Rose Crib 62–5
Draped Lace Crib 76–9
drapes 22–3
duck 46, 48
Duck's Bathtime 46–9

edible glue 13
Elegant Storks 19–23
elephant 74–5
embossing 44, 60, 61, 92
equipment 8–9

fabric effects 92–3
Fit for a Princess 58–61
flower paste 12–13
flower sprays 18, 98
flowers see blossoms, roses, flower
    sprays
font 50, 52
frilling 60–1, 64, 78–9, 92–3
fruit cake 10–11

Gift for Baby, A, 16–18
grapes 30

grass 75, 103
gum paste see flower paste

hearts 33, 70
hot-water bottle 69, 70

Jumbo Junior's Nap 72–5

lace designs 76, 78, 97, 98, 103;
    see also plastic lace
leaves 16, 22, 64, 88, 90
letters 18, 34, 96, 105–6
Little Angels 28–32

Madeira sponge cake 10
Making a Splash 50–3
modelling paste 13
modelling size guide 107

New Arrival 80–3

oriental stringwork 54, 56

pastillage 13
Pink Bootees 97–9
piping gel 53
plastic lace 9, 40, 76, 77
pleating 40–1, 60, 78, 84, 86, 93
pram 56–7, 101

presents 26

quantity guide 15

rabbits 70, 87, 96
rich fruit cake 10–11
rolled fondant see sugarpaste
roses 22, 62, 64, 88, 90
royal icing 11–12, 14–15

scallop design 54, 56
Sleepy Pals 69–71
smoke trail 83, 104
sponge cake 10
squares 34
storks 20, 23
sugarpaste 12, 14
suppliers 108–9

teddies 26–7, 36–9, 100
Teddies' Presents 24–7
templates 9, 100–6
textures 9, 80
toys 75
train 80, 82–3, 104
trees 75, 103
Twins' Slumber 84–7

Up, Up and Away Teddy 36–9

First published in 2002 by Murdoch Books UK Ltd

Merehurst is an imprint of Murdoch Books UK Ltd

Copyright 2002 © Murdoch Books UK Ltd

ISBN 1-85391-9446

A catalogue record of this book is available from the British Library

Commissioning Editor: Barbara Croxford

Editorial: Grapevine Publishing Services Ltd

Design: Maggie Aldred

Managing Editor: Anna Osborn

Design Manager: Helen Taylor

Cake photographer: Dominic Blackmore

Step photographer: Laurence Hudghton

Photo Librarian: Bobbie Leah

Templates: Chris King

CEO: Robert Oerton

Publisher: Catie Ziller

Production Manager: Lucy Byrne

International Sales Director: Kevin Lagden

Colour separation by Colourscan, Singapore

Printed by Tien Wah Press, Singapore

Murdoch Books UK Ltd
Ferry House, 51–57 Lacy Road,
Putney, London, SW15 1PR
United Kingdom
Tel: +44 (0)20 8355 1480
Fax: +44 (0)20 8355 1499
Murdoch Books UK Ltd is a subsidiary
of Murdoch Magazines Pty Ltd

UK Distribution
Macmillan Distribution Ltd
Houndmills, Brunell Road
Basingstoke, Hampshire RG21 6XS
United Kingdom
Tel: +44 (0)1256 302707
Fax: +44 (0)1256 351437
http://www.macmillan-mdl.co.uk

Murdoch Books®
GPO Box 1203
Sydney NSW 1045
Australia
Tel: +61 (0)2 4352 7025
Fax: +61 (0)2 4352 7026
Murdoch Books® is a trademark of
Murdoch Magazines Pty Ltd